Lecture Notes of the Institute for Computer Sciences, Social Informatics and Telecommunications Engineering 476

The LNICST series publishes ICST's conferences, symposia and workshops. It reports state-of-the-art results in areas related to the scope of the Institute.

LNICST reports state-of-the-art results in areas related to the scope of the Institute. The type of material published includes

- Proceedings (published in time for the respective event)
- Other edited monographs (such as project reports or invited volumes)

LNICST topics span the following areas:

- General Computer Science
- E-Economy
- E-Medicine
- Knowledge Management
- Multimedia
- Operations, Management and Policy
- Social Informatics
- Systems

Ivan Miguel Pires · Eftim Zdravevski ·
Nuno Cruz Garcia

Editors

Smart Objects and Technologies for Social Goods

8th EAI International Conference, GOODTECHS 2022
Aveiro, Portugal, November 16–18, 2022
Proceedings

 Springer

Editors
Ivan Miguel Pires (iD)
Instituto de Telecomunicações
Universidade da Beira Interior
Covilhã, Portugal

Eftim Zdravevski (iD)
Saints Cyril and Methodius
Skopje, North Macedonia

Nuno Cruz Garcia (iD)
University of Lisbon
Lisbon, Portugal

ISSN 1867-8211   ISSN 1867-822X (electronic)
Lecture Notes of the Institute for Computer Sciences, Social Informatics
and Telecommunications Engineering
ISBN 978-3-031-28812-8   ISBN 978-3-031-28813-5 (eBook)
https://doi.org/10.1007/978-3-031-28813-5

This Springer imprint is published by the registered company Springer Nature Switzerland AG
The registered company address is: Gewerbestrasse 11, 6330 Cham, Switzerland

Ivan Miguel Pires · Eftim Zdravevski ·
Nuno Cruz Garcia
Editors

Smart Objects and Technologies for Social Goods

8th EAI International Conference, GOODTECHS 2022
Aveiro, Portugal, November 16–18, 2022
Proceedings

 Springer

Editors
Ivan Miguel Pires (iD)
Instituto de Telecomunicações
Universidade da Beira Interior
Covilhã, Portugal

Eftim Zdravevski (iD)
Saints Cyril and Methodius
Skopje, North Macedonia

Nuno Cruz Garcia (iD)
University of Lisbon
Lisbon, Portugal

ISSN 1867-8211   ISSN 1867-822X (electronic)
Lecture Notes of the Institute for Computer Sciences, Social Informatics
and Telecommunications Engineering
ISBN 978-3-031-28812-8   ISBN 978-3-031-28813-5 (eBook)
https://doi.org/10.1007/978-3-031-28813-5

This Springer imprint is published by the registered company Springer Nature Switzerland AG
The registered company address is: Gewerbestrasse 11, 6330 Cham, Switzerland

Preface

This is the proceedings of the eighth edition of the European Alliance for Innovation (EAI) International Conference on Smart Objects and Technologies for Social Good (EAI GOODTECHS 2022), held on September 14–16, 2022. Researchers, developers, and practitioners from all over the world attended this conference to share their experiences in designing, implementing, deploying, operating, and evaluating smart objects and technologies for social benefit. Social goods are commodities and services that may be offered by nonprofit organizations, the government, or private businesses. Many people with unique needs, including seniors, athletes, and children, will benefit from the results of the conference. Health care, safety, sports, the environment, democracy, computer science, and human rights are all examples of social goods. The primary institution of the General Chair that provided and actively assisted in the organizing of this conference was the Instituto de Telecomunicaçes, which organized the conference.

The EAI GOODTECHS 2022 technical program featured 7 full papers in oral presentation sessions across all tracks. The main track, workshop tracks, and special session tracks were all included in the conference tracks. As a result, there were two conference tracks: "Main Track" and "Last-minute Track." In addition to the presentations of excellent technical papers, the technical program included five keynote speeches. Francesco Renna from INESC TEC in Porto, Pasquale Daponte from University of Sannio in Benevento, and Tiago Guerreiro from LASIGE Research Unit, Faculdade de Ciências, Universidade de Lisboa in Lisbon, Portugal, and Tech & People Lab in Lisbon, Portugal, delivered the three keynote sessions.

Coordination with the steering chair, Imrich Chlamtac was essential for the success of the conference. We sincerely appreciate his constant support and guidance. It was also a great pleasure to work with such an excellent organizing committee team for their hard work in organizing and supporting the conference. In particular, the Technical Program Committee, led by our TPC Co-Chairs, María Vanessa Villasana, Petre Lameski, and Susanna Spinsante who completed the peer-review process of technical papers and made a high-quality technical program. We are also grateful to Conference Managers, Kristina Havlickova for her support and all the authors who submitted their papers to the EAI GOODTECHS 2022 conference and workshops.

We are adamant that the GOODTECHS conference offers a suitable place for all researchers, developers, and practitioners to debate all science and technological issues pertinent to smart grids. In addition, based on the papers included in this collection, we anticipate that the subsequent GOODTECHS conference will be as fruitful and interesting.

Ivan Miguel Pires
Eftim Zdravevski
Nuno Cruz Garcia

Organization

Steering Committee

Imrich Chlamtac   Bruno Kessler Professor, University of Trento, Italy

Organizing Committee

General Chair

Ivan Miguel Pires   Instituto de Telecomunicações, Universidade da Beira Interior, Covilhã, Portugal

TPC Chair and Co-Chairs

María Vanessa Villasana   Centro Hospitalar Universitário Cova da Beira, Covilhã, Portugal

Petre Lameski   Saints Cyril and Methodius University, Skopje, Macedonia

Susanna Spinsante   Università Politecnica delle Marche, Ancona, Italy

Sponsorship and Exhibit Chair

Hanna Denysyuk   Universidade da Beira Interior, Covilhã, Portugal

Local Chair

Rogério Nogueira   Instituto de Telecomunicações, Universidade de Aveiro, Covilhã, Portugal

Workshops Chair

John Muñoz   University of Waterloo, Canada

Publicity and Social Media Chairs

Vania V. Estrela   Universidade Federal Fluminense, Brazil
Aleksandar Jevremovic   Singidunum University, Belgrade
José Morgado   Polytechnic Institute of Viseu, Portugal

Publications Chair

Eftim Zdravevski   Saints Cyril and Methodius University, Skopje,
                                             Macedonia

Web Chair

Nuno Cruz Garcia   Universidade de Lisboa, Portugal

Posters and PhD Track Chair

Sónia Sousa   Tallinn University, Estonia

Panels Chair

Rossitza Goleva   University Politehnica of Bucharest, Romania

Demos Chair

Ivan Chorbev   Saints Cyril and Methodius University, Skopje,
                                             Macedonia

Tutorials Chairs

Vladimir Trajkovikj   Saints Cyril and Methodius University, Skopje,
                                             Macedonia
Francisco Flórez-Revuelta   University of Alicante, Spain

Technical Program Committee

María Vanessa Villasana   Centro Hospitalar Universitário Cova da Beira,
                                             Covilhã, Portugal
Petre Lameski   Saints Cyril and Methodius University, Skopje,
                                             Macedonia

Susanna Spinsante	Università Politecnica delle Marche, Ancona, Italy
Eftim Zdravevski	Saints Cyril and Methodius University, Skopje, Macedonia
Carlos Albuquerque	Instituto Politécnico de Viseu, Viseu, Portugal
Ciprian Dobre	University Politehnica of Bucharest, Romania
Norberto Jorge Gonçalves	Universidade de Trás-os-Montes e Alto Douro, Vila Real, Portugal
Juliana Sá	Centro Hospitalar e Universitário do Porto, Porto, Portugal
José Lousado	Instituto Politécnico de Viseu, Viseu, Portugal
Lambros Lambrinos	Cyprus University of Technology, Cyprus
Constandinos Mavromoustakis	University of Nicosia, Cyprus
Arlindo Silva	Instituto Politécnico de Castelo Branco, Castelo Branco, Portugal
Madhusanka Liyanage	University College Dublin, Ireland
John Gialelis	University of Patras, Greece
Luis Augusto Silva	Universidad de Salamanca, Spain
Daniel Hernandez	Universidad Pontificia de Salamanca, Spain
Abdul Hannan	University of Management and Technology Taxila, Pakistan
Anvar Kabulov	National University of Uzbekistan, Uzbekistan
Islambek Saymanov	National University of Uzbekistan, Uzbekistan

Acknowledgement

This work is funded by FCT/MEC through national funds and, when applicable, co-funded by the FEDER-PT2020 partnership agreement under the project UIDB/50008/2020.

This article is based upon work from COST Action IC1303-AAPELE—Architectures, Algorithms, and Protocols for Enhanced Living Environments and COST Action CA16226–SHELD-ON—Indoor living space improvement: Smart Habitat for the Elderly, supported by COST (European Cooperation in Science and Technology). COST is a funding agency for research and innovation networks. Our Actions help connect research initiatives across Europe and enable scientists to grow their ideas by sharing them with their peers. It boosts their research, career, and innovation. More information in https://www.cost.eu.

Contents

Internet of Things

Multi-UAV Network Logistics Task Allocation Algorithm Based on Mean-Field-Type Game

Yao Hu[1](✉), Zhou Su[2], and Qichao Xu[1]

[1] School of Mechatronic Engineering and Automation, Shanghai University, Shanghai, China
quanhy422@163.com
[2] School of Cyber Science and Engineering, Xi'an Jiaotong University, Xi'an, China

Abstract. Unmanned aerial vehicles (UAVs) has become the vital driving force of logistics distribution development as an important carrier of advanced productivity. However, it is challenging to efficiently allocate logistics tasks on a large scale with the lowest energy consumption, considering the selfishness of UAVs. To tackle the above problem, we propose a mean field type game (MFTG) based logistics task allocation scheme in the multi-UAV networks. Specifically, we first develop a MFTG framework to fully model the interactions between the UAVs, the influence of aerodynamics and the features of tasks. Then, we propose the consensus-based bundle algorithm (CBBA) to provide a feasible and conflict-free solution to the multi-UAV network task allocation problem under multiple interactions in the dynamic environment. Extensive simulations are finally conducted, and results demonstrate that the proposed scheme can efficiently reduce the energy consumption of the multi-UAV network and provide users with high-quality task transportation service.

Keywords: Unmanned aerial vehicles (UAVs) · Mean-field-type game (MFTG) · Consensus-based bundle algorithm (CBBA) · Logistics task allocation

1 Introduction

With the development of e-commerce, one of the essential ways of logistics distribution in the future relays on unmanned aerial vehicles (UAVs) [1]. UAVs are suitable for remote areas and emergency delivery, which can effectively improve the efficiency of distribution, and achieve the reduction of labor and the transport costs. Therefore, the UAV-based supply delivery is becoming a potential development direction [2]. Realizing the full potential of UAVs may require a complete overhaul of logistics systems so that supply chains can have a chance to evolve from previous, old-fashioned standards to continuous, new fluid supply chains.

© ICST Institute for Computer Sciences, Social Informatics and Telecommunications Engineering 2023
Published by Springer Nature Switzerland AG 2023. All Rights Reserved
I. M. Pires et al. (Eds.): GOODTECHS 2022, LNICST 476, pp. 3–18, 2023.
https://doi.org/10.1007/978-3-031-28813-5_1

However, how to allocate logistics tasks such as the goods people buy online reasonably in a dynamic environment still faces many challenges. Specifically, UAVs have limited payloads and battery life. The number of UAVs in the multi-UAV network is limited, and the selfishness of UAVs have severe effects on the task allocation. Besides, due to the various user needs, UAVs need to tackle a variety of tasks. Therefore, an appropriate task allocation scheme should be devised to tackle the above issues and minimize the energy consumption.

In this paper, we propose a novel mean-field-type game (MFTG) framework with consensus-based bundle algorithm (CBBA) in the multi-UAV network to allocate the tasks and minimize the energy consumption. Specifically, the framework is first proposed to model the interactions between the UAVs in the static environment, which can motivate the participation of the UAVs and determine the optimal task allocation strategy to minimize the energy consumption. Furthermore, for lack of the knowledge on interactions between UAVs in dynamic network scenarios, the CBBA is used to decide the optimal task allocation strategy through trial and error under multiple interactions. The main contributions of this paper are as follows:

(1) We build an air-to-ground task allocation model in the multi-UAVs network for logistics distribution, considering aerodynamic factors, load and data transmission consumption and the time-to-live (TTL) of the tasks.
(2) We model the problem of task allocation as a MFTG framework to fully consider the impact of UAVs' selfishness on task allocation with the state equation.
(3) Without knowing the utility parameters between UAVs, the CBBA is utilized into the MFTG framework to minimize the energy consumption of task allocation while ensuring timely service in the dynamic environment.

The rest of this paper is organized as follows. Section 2 reviews the related work. The system model is introduced in Sect. 3. Section 4 presents the problem formulation and Sect. 5 analyzes the optimal strategy for static mean-field-type game. The consensus-based bundle algorithm based optimal strategy decision is expounded in Sect. 6. Performance evaluation is shown in Sect. 7 and the conclusion is summarized in Sect. 8.

2   Related Work

2.1   Mean-Field-Type Game in UAVs

In recent years, the mean-field-type game theory in UAVs has attracted wide attention from academic research to life application. Chen et al. [3] investigated the resource management problem for large-scale UAV communication networks and discussed the potential applications. Li et al. [4] formulated the power control problem of the UAVs as a discrete mean-field game and transformed it into a Markov decision process by simulating the interactions among a large number of UAVs to obtain an equilibrium solution. It can be seen that there are few studies in the existing literature on solving the task allocation problem in multi-UAVs networks by using the mean-field-type game theory with the CBBA algorithm.

2.2 Incentives with Consensus-Based Bundle Algorithm

With the development of distributed algorithms, the CBBA has been studied extensively. Zitouni *et al.* [5] devised a distributed approach to multi-robot task assignment by combining CBBA with ant colony algorithm. To solve the potential problems of information transmission quality and energy consumption in wireless sensor network, Chen *et al.* [6] adopted the consensus-based bundle algorithm to generate corresponding task assignment schedules. However, the considerations of the UAVs' interactions and the network state update in the multi-UAVs networks are still insufficient.

Different from existing works, the proposed scheme studies the task allocation in the multi-UAVs network. The internal (e.g., selfishness and the battery life of UAVs) and external(e.g., aerodynamics and the TTL of tasks) factors of the network are jointly considered in the dynamic environment to improve the efficiency of delivery. In addition, the CBBA is employed to acquire the optimal tasks allocation strategy of UAVs in the dynamic MFTG.

3 System Model

In this section, we introduce the system model including network model, task model, motion model and communication model.

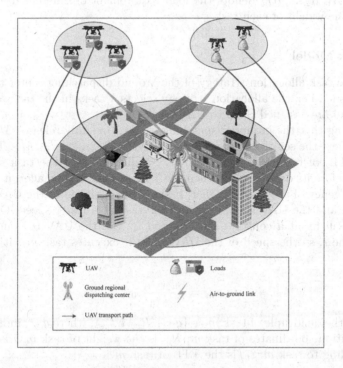

Fig. 1. System model.

3.1   Network Model

In this paper, we consider an intelligent logistics model, as shown in Fig. 1, which includes a ground dispatching center, multiple UAVs, and some users.

Ground Dispatching Center. The ground dispatching center collects information such as geographical location, the demand and TTL of distribution tasks, and publishes them to the multi-UAV network.

UAVs. UAVs submit the latest location information to the ground dispatching center, and obtain the released task information through the dispatching center. The set of UAVs is denoted as $\mathcal{U} = \{1, 2, ..., u, ..., U\}$. UAVs are equipped with various types of sensors to collect sensing data from users on the ground. Let $\mathcal{L} = \{L_1, L_2, ..., L_U\}$ denote the maximum load constraint of different UAVs. Define the state of UAV u at time t as $\mathbf{x}_u = \{q_u(t), E_{u,remain}(t)\}$, where $q_u(t)$ and $E_{u,remain}(t)$ are the position coordinates and the remaining energy of UAV u at time t, respectively.

Users. Users submit their geographical location and task information to the ground dispatching center. The set of users is denoted as $\mathcal{I} = \{1, 2, ..., i, ..., I\}$. Let $\mathcal{R} = \{R_1, R_2, ..., R_I\}$ denote the load requirement of different users, which represent the weight of each task.

3.2   Task Model

Defined the task allocation strategy of the ground dispatching center to UAV u at time t is $\mathbf{s}_u$, i.e., the allocation strategy selects k tasks in the task set $\mathcal{M}$ are selected and are assigned them to UAV u.

Assuming that the ground dispatching center randomly releases M tasks at time t_0, where the set of tasks is denoted as $\mathcal{M} = \{1, 2, ..., m, ..., M\}$. The time-to-live (TTL) of task m is denoted by t_m, indicating that the task should be executed before its deadline [7]. When the TTL of task m is smaller, it indicates that the urgency of the task is higher. It should be assigned to the UAV as soon as possible and the UAV should execute the task at a faster speed. Otherwise, the UAV will fly at a constant initial speed v_0. Set the UAV to complete the task at time t, so the speed of the UAV when it executes task m with TTL of t_m is

$$v_m = \frac{t_m - t_0}{t - t_0} v_0 \tag{1}$$

Define the quadruple of task m as $\{q_i(t), R_m, i, t_m\}$, where $q_i(t)$ indicates the target position coordinates of task m. R_m is the weight of task m. i is the user corresponding to task m. t_m is the TTL of task m.

3.3 Motion Model

We consider that UAVs fly at a constant altitude, and the position coordinates of UAV u is $q_u(t) = [x_u(t), y_u(t), H]$, where $x_u(t)$ and $y_u(t)$ are the horizontal and vertical coordinates of UAV u, and H is the altitude of UAV u. The position coordinates of user i is $q_i(t) = [x_i(t), y_i(t), 0]$. Therefore, the distance between UAV u and user i is

$$d_{u,i} = \sqrt{[x_u(t) - x_i(t)^2] + [y_u(t) - y_i(t)^2] + H^2} \qquad (2)$$

Assuming that UAVs fly at a constant speed, the flight time of the UAV u for executing task m is

$$t_m^u = \frac{\sqrt{[x_u(t) - x_i(t)^2] + [y_u(t) - y_i(t)^2] + H^2}}{v_m} \qquad (3)$$

and the position change trend of UAV u at time t is expressed by state dynamic equation $\mathbf{x}'(t)$ [14].

$$\mathbf{x}'_u(t) = \theta \mathbf{x_u}(t) + \sum_{u=1}^{U} \lambda_u \mathbf{s}_u(t) \qquad (4)$$

where θ and λ_u indicate the impact of the environment in the current state and the speed of UAV u relative to other UAVs, respectively.

3.4 Communication Model

The LoS channel model provides a practical approximation for the air-to-ground (A2G) channel transmission [8]. Therefore, the channel gain between UAV u and user i is

$$g_{ui}(t) = \frac{g_0}{[(x_u(t) - x_i(t)]^2 + [y_u(t) - y_i(t)]^2 + H^2} \qquad (5)$$

where g_0 represents the channel gain per unit distance.

In the process of logistics delivery, information such as distribution status, geographical location and expected arrival time is continuously communicated with users, so the signal-to-noise ratio between UAV u and user i [8] is

$$\varphi_{ui} = \frac{g_{ui}(t)p_u}{\sum_{u' \in \mathcal{U} \backslash u} g_{u'i}(t)p_{u'} + \sigma^2} \qquad (6)$$

where p_u is the downlink transmission power of UAV u. $\sum_{u' \in \mathcal{U} \backslash u} g_{u'i}(t)p_{u'}$ is the interference power from all UAVs except UAV u. σ^2 denotes the Gaussian noise.

The data transmission rate is characterized as

$$r_{ui} = \omega \log_2 (1 + \varphi_{ui}) \qquad (7)$$

where ω is the bandwidth allocated to UAV u.

4   Problem Formulation

4.1   Utility Function

The energy consumption of UAVs is determined by three parts, including the fight energy consumption, the data transmission consumption and the load consumption. We use the cost function of energy consumption to represent the utility function, and achieve the lowest energy consumption by minimizing the utility function.

Flight Energy Consumption. [9]

$$c_{1,u} = \int_0^{t_m^u} [a_1(1 + a_2 v_m^2) + a_3(\sqrt{1 + \frac{v_m^4}{4a_4^2}} - \frac{v_m^2}{2a_4})^{\frac{1}{2}}]dt \tag{8}$$

where a_1 and a_2 are the parameters based on the UAV weight and air density. a_3 is the UAV rotor parameters and a_4 is the coefficient of air resistance.

Data Transmission Consumption. In the process of executing tasks, each UAV must ensure the communication quality. Meanwhile, data transmission also consumes a significant amount of energy. As such, the data transmission consumption of UAV u is given by

$$c_{2,u} = p_u \frac{D}{r_{ui}} \tag{9}$$

where D is the size of the transmitted data.

Load Cost. The UAV performing the task needs to meet the weight required of the task. And the load cost of UAV u performing task m is

$$c_{3,u} = P_m t_m^u \tag{10}$$

where P_m is the load power of UAV for task m.

Combining (8), (9) and (10), the cost function of UAV u is expressed as

$$c_u = \sum_{m=1}^{M} Z_{u,m}(\omega_1 c_{1,u} + \omega_2 c_{2,u} + \omega_3 c_{3,u}) \tag{11}$$

where $Z_{u,m}$ is a binary variable. When $Z_{u,m} = 1$, it indicates that task m is allocated to UAV u; otherwise, $Z_{u,m} = 0$. $\omega_1, \omega_2, \omega_3$ are the weighting parameter.

Therefore, the utility function of UAV u is

$$U_u(\mathbf{x}_u, \mathbf{s}_u) = c_u = \sum_{m=1}^{M} Z_{u,m}(\omega_1 c_{1,u} + \omega_2 c_{2,u} + \omega_3 c_{3,u})$$

$$= \sum_{m=1}^{M} Z_{u,m}(\omega_1 \int_0^{t_m^u} [a_1(1 + a_2 v_m^2)$$

$$+ a_3(\sqrt{1 + \frac{v_m^4}{4a_4^2} - \frac{v_m^2}{2a_4}})^{\frac{1}{2}}]dt + \omega_2 p_u \frac{D}{r_{ui}} + \omega_3 P_m t_m^u) \qquad (12)$$

$$= \sum_{m=1}^{M} Z_{u,m}(\omega_1 \int_0^{\frac{\sqrt{[x_u(t)-x_i(t)^2]+[y_u(t)-y_i(t)^2]+H^2}}{v_m}} [a_1(1 + a_2 v_m^2)$$

$$+ a_3(\sqrt{1 + \frac{v_m^4}{4a_4^2} - \frac{v_m^2}{2a_4}})^{\frac{1}{2}}]dt + \omega_2 p_u \frac{D}{r_{ui}}$$

$$+ \omega_3 P_m \frac{\sqrt{[x_u(t) - x_i(t)^2] + [y_u(t) - y_i(t)^2] + H^2}}{v_m})$$

4.2 Optimization Problem

With the above description, a task allocation strategy to achieve the lowest energy consumption is obtained by minimizing the utility function. As such, the optimization problem is introduced.

Problem 1: The optimization problem for minimizing the energy consumption of the UAV can be formulated as

$$min \quad U_u(\mathbf{x}_u, \mathbf{s}_u),$$

$$s.t. \quad t_0 \leq t < t_m. \quad \forall m \in \mathcal{M}$$

$$c_u \leq E_{u,remain}(t). \quad \forall u \in \mathcal{U}$$

$$\sum_{u=1}^{U} Z_{u,m} \leq 1. \quad \forall u \in \mathcal{U} \qquad (13)$$

$$\sum_{m=1}^{M} Z_{u,m} \leq L_u. \quad \forall u \in \mathcal{U}, \forall m \in \mathcal{M}$$

The proposed optimization problem is a NP-hard problem, which uses the MFTG to decompose the problem into the minimization problem of each UAV to realize the overall minimization. Considering the interactions between UAV's in the game, a new utility function is constructed by means of the mean-field value.

5 Static Mean-Field-Type Game Analysis

In this section, we construct the MFTG framework and obtain the equilibrium solution. The framework allows UAVs, as the multi-agents, to perform heterogeneous behaviors. The selfish behavior of any UAV in the network will affect the cost of other agents in the game. We analyze the optimal strategy of UAVs with the static MTFG, where the parameters of the game are public knowledge to all UAVs. The mean-field value of state and the mean-field value of strategy are shown in (14), (15), respectively.

$$\bar{\mathbf{x}}(t) = \frac{\sum_{u=1}^{U} \mathbf{x}_u(t)}{U} \tag{14}$$

$$\bar{\mathbf{s}}(t) = \frac{\sum_{u=1}^{U} \mathbf{s}_u(t)}{U} \tag{15}$$

At the final time $t = t_m^u$, considering the state of the UAV u, the terminal cost function can be expressed as

$$\Phi_u(\mathbf{x}(t_m^u), t_m^u) = \omega_4 E_{u,remain}^2(t_m^u) \tag{16}$$

The terminal function can be rewritten as

$$\Phi_u(\mathbf{x}_u, \bar{\mathbf{x}}, t_m^u) = \omega_4[\mathbf{x}_u^2(t_m^u) + \bar{\mathbf{x}}^2(t_m^u)] \tag{17}$$

According to the mean-field values, the utility function can be rewritten as

$$\begin{aligned}
\widetilde{U}_u(\mathbf{s}) &= U_u(\mathbf{x}_u, \bar{\mathbf{x}}, \mathbf{s}_u, \bar{\mathbf{s}}, t) + \Phi_u(\mathbf{x}(t_m^u), t_m^u) \\
&= \sum_{m=1}^{M} Z_{u,m}\{\omega_1[(c_{1,u}(\mathbf{x}_u, \mathbf{s}_u, t) + c_{1,u}(\mathbf{x}_u, \bar{\mathbf{x}}, \mathbf{s}_u, \bar{\mathbf{s}}, t)] \\
&\quad + \omega_2[c_{2,u}(\mathbf{x}_u, \mathbf{s}_u, t) + (c_{2,u}(\mathbf{x}_u, \bar{\mathbf{x}}, \mathbf{s}_u, \bar{\mathbf{s}}, t)] \\
&\quad + \omega_3[c_{3,u}(\mathbf{x}_u, \mathbf{s}_u, t) + (c_{3,u}(\mathbf{x}_u, \bar{\mathbf{x}}, \mathbf{s}_u, \bar{\mathbf{s}}, t)] + \Phi_u(\mathbf{x}(t_m^u), t_m^u)\}
\end{aligned} \tag{18}$$

Meanwhile, according to the MFTG model, the state dynamics equation can be rewritten as

$$d\mathbf{x}(t) = \theta\mathbf{x}(t) + \sum_{u=1}^{U} \lambda_u \mathbf{s}_u(t) + \bar{\theta}\bar{\mathbf{x}}(t) + \sum_{u=1}^{U} \bar{\lambda}_u \bar{\mathbf{s}}_u(t))dt + \mu dB(t) \tag{19}$$

where $B(t)$ represents a random Brownian process. μ is a parameter to measure Brownian process. $\bar{\theta}$ and $\bar{\lambda}_u$ respectively represent the mean of environmental impact factors and the mean of relative speed.

Hence, the MFTG problem is formulated in Problem 2.

Problem 2 (MFTG Problem): Consider the following problem:

$$\begin{cases} \inf_{\mathbf{s}_u \in \mathbf{S}_u} \mathbb{E}[\widetilde{U}_u(\mathbf{s})] = \inf_{\mathbf{s}_u \in \mathbf{S}_u} \mathbb{E}[\int_0^{t_u^m} U_u(\mathbf{x}_u, \bar{\mathbf{x}}, \mathbf{s}_u, \bar{\mathbf{s}}, t)dt + \Phi_u(\mathbf{x}_u, \bar{\mathbf{x}}, t_m^u)] \\ dx(t) = \theta x(t) + \sum_{u=1}^{U} \lambda_u \mathbf{s}_u(t) + \bar{\theta}\bar{\mathbf{x}}(t) + \sum_{u=1}^{U} \bar{\lambda}_u \bar{\mathbf{s}}(t))dt + \mu dB(t) \end{cases} \tag{20}$$

Definition 1. (*MFTG Best Response*): Any feasible strategy $\mathbf{s}_u^* \in \mathbf{S}_u$ satisfying the infimum in (20) is the best response strategy of decision maker $u \in \mathcal{U}$ against the others decision makers strategies $\mathbf{s}_{-u} \in \prod_{u' \in \mathcal{U} \setminus \{u\}} \mathbf{S}_u$. The set of strategies is given by $BR_u : \mathbf{u}_{-u} \prod_{u' \in \mathcal{U} \setminus \{u\}} \mathbf{S}_u \rightarrow 2^{\mathbf{S}_u}$, where $2^{\mathbf{S}_u}$ is the power set of all the possible subsets of $\mathbf{S}_u$.

Definition 2. (*MFTG Nash Equilibrium*): The profile of any feasible strategy $[\mathbf{s}_u^*, ..., \mathbf{s}_U^*] \in \prod_{u' \in \mathcal{U}} \mathbf{S}_u$ that optimizes $\mathbf{s}_u^* \in BR_u(\mathbf{s}_{-u}^*)$ for every $\mathbb{E}[\mathbf{x}^*(t)]$ is a mean-field-type Nash equilibrium of the MFTG, as Eq. (21) shows

$$\widetilde{U}_u(\mathbf{s}_u^*, \mathbf{s}_{-u}^*) \leq \widetilde{U}_u(\mathbf{s}_u, \mathbf{u}_{-u}^*) \tag{21}$$

The mean-field-type game problem of interest in this section is achieve that u is the best response to problem 3.2 for every UAV by finding and representing processes such as $[\mathbf{x}^*, \mathbf{s}^*, \mathbb{E}[\mathbf{x}^*], \mathbb{E}[\mathbf{s}^*]]$. It suggests that the Nash equilibrium is a fixed point for the best response $[BR = (BR_1, BR_2, ..., BR_U)]$, where each BR_U is the best response corresponding to UAV u.

Proposition 1. The optimal strategy is given by:

$$\mathbf{s}_u^* = -\beta_u \frac{(b_u + \bar{b}_u)}{(r_u + \bar{r}_u)} \mathbb{E}[\mathbf{x}] - \alpha_u \frac{b_u}{r_u} (\mathbf{x} - \mathbb{E}[\mathbf{x}]) \tag{22}$$

Proof: This proof is presented in [10].

6 Consensus-Based Bundle Algorithm Based Optimal Strategy Decision for Dynamic MFTG

In this section, we analyze the dynamic MFTG in the multi-UAVs, where the interactions between UAVs are repeatedly conducted over time. In the dynamic MFTG game, the utility parameters between UAVs are private in reality and cannot be fully understood by all UAVs. The UAVs interact with each other several times, to find the optimal strategy through trial and error. CBBA can model the UAVs under multiple interactions.

6.1 Score Function

The interactions between UAVs of the task allocation problem is simplified into mean-field value interaction by the MFTG theory. Therefore, the utility function is updated to score function to measure the effect of task allocation strategy in dynamic MTFG. The score function should be modified as

$$\hat{U}_u(\mathbf{x}_u, \mathbf{s}_u, \mathbf{p}_u) = U_u(\mathbf{x}_u, \bar{\mathbf{x}}, \mathbf{s}_u, \bar{\mathbf{x}}, t) + F_0 + e^{-\mu_u(t_u - t_0)}(F - F_0)X_{tw} \tag{23}$$

where F_0 is the fixed reward to ensure the total score is non-negative and $(F - F_0)$ is the discount reward of the task. μ_u is the discount factor. X_{tw} is the binary variable that indicates if the task plan satisfies the TTL constrain.

6.2   Task Allocation Model

The objective of CBBA is to obtain feasible and conflict-free task allocation solution when maximizes the score function [11]. The problem is expressed as follows:

$$
\begin{aligned}
max \quad & \hat{U}_u(\mathbf{x}_u, \mathbf{s}_u, \mathbf{p}_u) Z_{u,m}, \\
s.t. \quad & t_0 \le t < t_0 + t_m. \quad \forall m \in \mathcal{M} \\
& c_u \le E_{u,remain}(t). \quad \forall u \in \mathcal{U} \\
& \sum_{u=1}^{U} Z_{u,m} \le 1. \quad \forall u \in \mathcal{U} \\
& \sum_{m=1}^{M} Z_{u,m} \le L_u. \quad \forall u \in \mathcal{U}, \forall m \in \mathcal{M} \\
& \sum_{u=1}^{U} \sum_{m=1}^{M} Z_{u,m} = min\{\mathcal{U}, \mathcal{M}, R_m\}.
\end{aligned}
\tag{24}
$$

where $\mathbf{p}_u$ is the order in which the UAV u executes the assigned tasks.

6.3   Consensus-Based Bundle Algorithm

The process of consensus-based bundle algorithm (CBBA) solving the multi-tasks allocation problem is divided into two phases: bundle construction and conflict resolution phases [12].

Bundle Construction. In the process of task allocation, the UAV u needs to store and update the following information structure:

– Bundle list $\mathbf{b}_u \in (\mathcal{M} \cup \{\emptyset\})^{L_u}$: indicates that tasks are sorted in the order in which they are added to packages.
– Path list $\mathbf{p}_u \in (\mathcal{M} \cup \{\emptyset\})^{L_u}$: refers to the optimal task execution sequence.
– Winner list $\mathbf{z}_u \in (\mathcal{U} \cup \{\emptyset\})^{\mathcal{M}}$: means the highest bid for task m of corresponding UAV in local information.
– Winning bid list $y_u \in (R_+)^{\mathcal{M}}$: represents the highest bid the UAV u considering task m.
– Time stamp $\mathbf{t}_u \in (R)^{\mathcal{U}}$: is the update time of information received by the UAV u from the other members of the network.

We adopt a diminishing marginal gain function to make the CBBA converge [13]. $S_u^{\mathbf{p}_i \oplus_n m}$ represents the reward value of the UAV u executing the task m which is inserted into the nth position.

$$
c_{um} = max S_u^{\mathbf{p}_u \oplus_n m} - S_u^{\mathbf{p}_u}, \quad u \notin \mathbf{p}_u
\tag{25}
$$

$$c_{um}(\mathbf{b}_u) \geq c_{um}(\mathbf{b}_u \bigoplus{}_{end}\mathbf{b}) \tag{26}$$

The bundle construction of UAV u is implemented by Algorithm 1. $S_u^{\mathbf{p}_u}$ represents the total reward value of the UAV u executing the task along its path $\mathbf{p}_u$, where its initial value is 0.

Algorithm 1. CBBA phase 1 for UAV u at iteration t

Input: $\mathbf{b}_u(t-1), \mathbf{p}_u(t-1), \mathbf{z}_u(t-1), \mathbf{y}_u(t-1)$
Output: $\mathbf{b}_u(t), \mathbf{p}_u(t), \mathbf{z}_u(t), \mathbf{y}_u(t)$

1: $\mathbf{b}_u(t) = \mathbf{b}_u(t-1), \mathbf{p}_u(t) = \mathbf{p}_u(t-1)$
2: $\mathbf{z}_u(t) = \mathbf{z}_u(t-1), \mathbf{y}_u(t) = \mathbf{y}_u(t-1)$
3: **while** $|\mathbf{b}_u(t)| < R_m$ **do**
4:     $c_{um} = max_{u \leq |\mathbf{p}_u|} S_u^{\mathbf{p}_u \oplus_n m} - S_u^{\mathbf{p}_u}, \quad m \notin \mathbf{p}_u$
5:     $h_{um} = \amalg(c_{um} > y_{um})$
6:     $\mathcal{M}_u = \operatorname{argmax}_u(c_{um}(\mathbf{b}_u) \times h_{um})$
7:     $n_{u,\mathcal{M}_u} = \operatorname{argmax}_u S_u^{\mathbf{p}_u \oplus_n \mathcal{M}_u}$
8:     $\mathbf{b}_u = \mathbf{b}_u \bigoplus_{end}\{\mathcal{M}_u\}$
9:     $\mathbf{b}_u = \mathbf{b}_u \bigoplus_{n_{u,\mathcal{M}_u}}\{\mathcal{M}_u\}$
10:    $y_{u,\mathcal{M}_u}(t) = c_{u,\mathcal{M}_u}, z_{u,\mathcal{M}_u} = u$
11: **end while**

The process of bundle construction continues among the tasks until the construction of the task bundle list is completed, that is, the number of tasks in the bundle list reaches the upper limit of the number of tasks that UAVs can handle, or reaches the number of all tasks that need to be handled.

Conflict Resolution. After the task bundle construction process is completed, the UAV shares the bundle list and other information with the adjacent UAVs, and the corresponding task information is updated according to certain action rules to obtain the conflict-free task allocation. UAV u can take the following three actions on task m after receiving the message assigned by neighboring UAV j:

- Update: $y_{um} = y_{jm}, z_{um} = z_{jm}$;
- Reset: $y_{um} = 0, z_{um} = \emptyset$;
- Leave: $y_{um} = y_{um}, z_{um} = z_{um}$.

The conflict resolution of UAV u is implemented by Algorithm 2. After the multiple rounds of communications and negotiations through the conflict resolution, the winner list and the winning bid list will achieve a consensus [12].

7   Performance Evaluation

7.1   Simulation Setup

In the simulation scenario, there is a 600×600 m^2 terrain with one ground dispatching center. The flight height of all UAVs is set to 500 m. The positions of the tasks and the UAVs are randomly distributed. The number of UAVs is $U = 5$, and the number of tasks are $M = 10, 15, 20, 25$. The constant initial speed of UAVs is set to 80 m/s. The weighting parameters in the utility function are $\omega_1 = \omega_2 = \omega_3 = 1/3$. The parameters in the score function are $\mu_u = 0.1$, $F_0 = 10$ and $F = 100$ [13].

Algorithm 2. CBBA phase 2 for UAV u at iteration t

Input: $\mathbf{b}_u, \mathbf{p}_u, \mathbf{z}_u, \mathbf{y}_u, \mathbf{t}_u$
Output: $\mathbf{B}_u, \mathbf{P}_u, \mathbf{Z}_u, \mathbf{Y}_u, \mathbf{t}_u$

1: $\mathbf{B}_u = \mathbf{b}_u, \mathbf{P}_u = \mathbf{p}_u$
2: $\mathbf{Y}_u = \mathbf{y}_u \oplus 0, \mathbf{Z}_u = \mathbf{z}_u \oplus \emptyset$
3: $\mathcal{M}_{u,reset} = \emptyset$
4: if $CM(u, m_*) = 1$ then
5:     for $m \in \mathbf{B}_u$ do
6:         if $t_u * m$ overlaps with $[t_0, t_{m*}]$ then
7:             $\mathcal{M}_{u,reset} = \mathcal{M}_{u,reset} \bigcup \{u\}$
8:             $\mathbf{D}_{u,reset}(u) = S(\mathbf{p}_u) + S_u^{\mathbf{P}_u \oplus_n m^*}$
9:         end if
10:     end for
11:     if $\mathcal{M}_{u,reset} \neq \emptyset$ then
12:         $m_{u,reset} = argmin_u \mathbf{D}_{u,reset}$
13:         $\mathbf{B}_u = \mathbf{B}_u \ominus \{u_{u,reset}\}, \mathbf{P}_u = \mathbf{P}_u \ominus \{m_{u,reset}\}$
14:         $\mathbf{Y}_{u,reset} = 0, \mathbf{Z}_{u,reset} = \emptyset, \mathbf{t}_{u,reset} = 0$
15:     end if
16: end if
17: Phase 2: conflict resolution
18: Phase 1: bundle construction $(\mathbf{B}_u, \mathbf{P}_u, \mathbf{Z}_u, \mathbf{Y}_u, \mathbf{t}_u)$
19: Phase 2: conflict resolution

7.2   Numerical Results

Figure 2 shows the energy consumption of UAVs with different number of tasks. As can be seen from Fig. 2, the proposed scheme has lower energy consumption. In the proposed scheme, each UAV selects the optimal strategy based on the MFTG, which can effectively reduce the energy consumption. In the random option algorithm, UAVs choose the strategy randomly, leading to a higher energy consumption. As for the greedy algorithm, UAVs only focus on the shortest path while ignore the characteristics of different tasks.

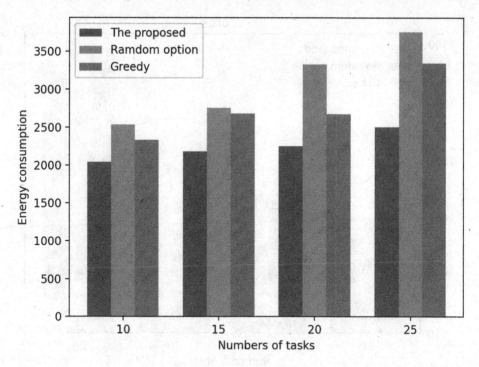

Fig. 2. The energy consumption with different numbers of tasks.

Figure 3 shows the scores of UAVs in a number of different tasks. As shown in Fig. 3, the proposed scheme can obtain a higher score. This is because the scheme takes into account not only the selfishness of UAVs, but also the interactions between them.

Figure 4 shows the equality capability index of UAVs in terms of different amounts of tasks. According to the equalization ability index in the engineering system, the balanced and reasonable task allocation of the three algorithms is measured. Define CP_i as the equality capability index, which is

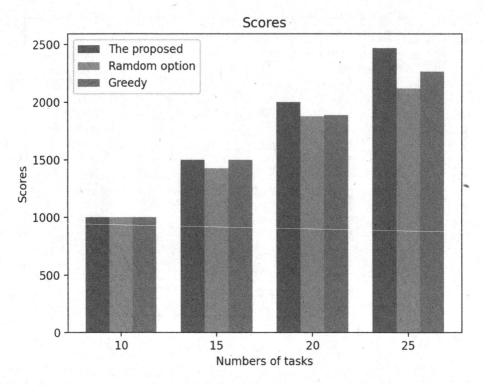

Fig. 3. The scores with different numbers of tasks.

$$CP_i = \frac{k - \bar{m}}{3\sigma_m}, \tag{27}$$

where k is the number of tasks allocated to UAV u. $\bar{m}$ is the average number of tasks allocated to each UAV. σ_m is The standard deviation. When $0.67 < CP_i < 1$, the allocation is relatively balanced. From Fig. 3, we can observe that the proposed scheme can obtain a more balanced allocation. This is because the proposed scheme achieve a consensus on the tasks through the conflict resolution.

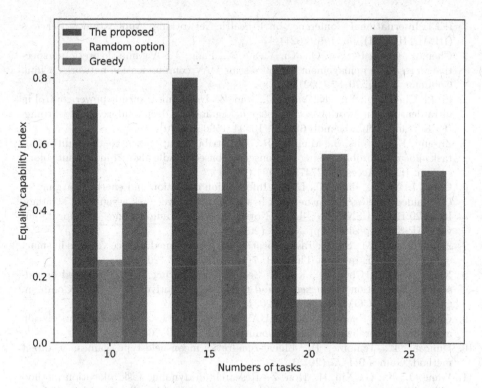

Fig. 4. The equality capability index with different numbers of tasks.

8   Conclusion

In this paper, we have presented a novel logistics task allocation scheme in the multi-UAV network. First, to model interactions between UAVs, a static MTFG framework is proposed to consider the selfishness and external aerodynamic factors, where all the UAVs can obtain the minimum energy consumption. Then, we have employed the CBBA to obtain the optimal strategy for each UAV in the dynamic environment. At last, the simulation results show that the proposed scheme can efficiently reduce the energy consumption of UAVs and allocation the tasks. For the future work, the variety of task model and deep reinforcement learning method for path planning will be investigated.

References

1. Wu, J., Su, X.: UAV task assignment algorithm based on splitting and reorganization. In: IEEE International Conferences on Ubiquitous Computing & Communications (IUCC) and Data Science and Computational Intelligence (DSCI) and Smart Computing. Networking and Services (SmartCNS), vol. 2019, pp. 35–42 (2019)
2. Huang, Y., Han, H., Zhang, B., Su, X. Gong, Z.:Supply distribution center planning in UAV-based logistics networks for post-disaster supply delivery. In: 2020

IEEE International Conference on E-health Networking, Application & Services (HEALTHCOM), pp. 1–6 (2021)

3. Chen, J., Chen, P., Wu, Q., Xu, Y., Qi, N., Fang, T.: A game-theoretic perspective on resource management for large-scale UAV communication networks. China Commun. **18**(1), 70–87 (2021)

4. Li, L., Cheng, Q., Xue, K., Yang, C., Han, Z.: Downlink transmit power control in ultra-dense uav network based on mean field game and deep reinforcement learning. IEEE Trans. Veh. Technol. **69**(12), 15594–15605 (2020)

5. Zitouni, F., Harous, S., Maamri, R.: A distributed approach to the multi-robot task allocation problem using the consensus-based bundle algorithm and ant colony system. IEEE Access **8**, 27479–27494 (2020)

6. Chen, J., Ye, F., Jiang, T., Li, Y.: Information collection and energy charging for UAV-aided wireless sensor network based on a two-layer task assignment strategy. In: 2020 IEEE USNC-CNC-URSI North American Radio Science Meeting (Joint with AP-S Symposium), pp. 55–56 (2020)

7. Zhang, J., Dai, M., Su, Z.: Task allocation with unmanned surface vehicles in smart ocean IoT. IEEE Internet Things J. **7**(10), 9702–9713 (2020)

8. Xie, L., Su, Z., Chen, N., Xu, Q.: Secure data sharing in UAV-assisted crowd-sensing: integration of blockchain and reputation incentive. IEEE Glob. Commun. Conf. (GLOBECOM) **2021**, 1–6 (2021)

9. Gao, N., et al.: Energy model for UAV communications: experimental validation and model generalization. China Commun. **18**(7), 253–264 (2021)

10. Duncan, T., Tembine, H.: Linear-quadratic mean-field-type games: a direct method. Games **9**(1), 7 (2018)

11. Wang, J., Jia, G., Xin, H., Hon, Z.: Research on dynamic task allocation method of heterogeneous multi-UAV based on consensus based bundle algorithm. Chinese Autom. Congr. (CAC) **2020**, 2214–2219 (2020)

12. Zhang, Y., Feng, W., Shi, G., et al.: UAV swarm mission planning in dynamic environment using consensus-based bundle algorithm. Sensors **20**(8), 2307 (2020)

13. Chen, J., et al.: Consensus-based bundle algorithm with local replanning for heterogeneous multi-UAV system in the time-sensitive and dynamic environment. J. Supercomput. **78**(2), 1712–1740 (2022)

14. Sun, Y., et al.: Inhomogeneous multi-UAV aerial base stations deployment: a mean-field-type game approach. In: 2019 15th International Wireless Communications & Mobile Computing Conference (IWCMC). IEEE (2019)

On the Influence of Grid Cell Size on Taxi Demand Prediction

Merlin Korth[1]([✉]) [iD], Sören Schleibaum[1] [iD], Jörg P. Müller[1] [iD],
and Rüdiger Ehlers[2] [iD]

[1] Department of Informatics, Clausthal University of Technology,
Julius-Albert-Straße 4, 38678 Clausthal-Zellerfeld, Germany
{merlin.korth,soeren.schleibaum,joerg.mueller}@tu-clausthal.de
[2] Institute for Software and Systems Engineering, Clausthal University of
Technology, Julius-Albert-Straße 4, 38678 Clausthal-Zellerfeld, Germany
ruediger.ehlers@tu-clausthal.de

Abstract. Accurate taxi demand prediction has the potential to increase customer satisfaction and hence the usage of ride-sharing by predicting the number of taxis needed at a certain place and time. When reviewing the related work on demand prediction, we observed that in taxi demand prediction different grid topologies – e.g. rectangular subdivisions of an area – and sizes are applied. However, it is not clear how and why the grid cells are configured the way they are and a systematic comparison of different topologies and sizes as regards their influence on urban demand prediction is lacking.

In this paper, we compare the influence of different grid cell sizes – 250 m, 500 m, and 1000 m – on the prediction accuracy of different types of deep learning-based taxi demand prediction approaches, such as convolutional neural networks, recurrent neural networks, and graph neural networks. Therefore, we select five deep learning-based approaches from related work and evaluate their performance on the New York City TLC taxi trip dataset and three different evaluation metrics. Our results show that approaches with a grid cell of size 1000 m and 500 m achieve a higher prediction accuracy. Furthermore, we propose to consider the grid cell size as a tunable parameter in demand prediction models.

Keywords: Taxi demand prediction · Grid cell size · Deep learning

1 Introduction

About 99% of the world's population breathes air that does not meet the World Health Organizations' air quality guidelines [23]. A major cause is urbanization, which includes the concentration of pollution sources in a relatively small

This work was in part supported by the Deutsche Forschungsgemeinschaft under grant 227198829/GRK1931. The SocialCars Research Training Group focuses on future mobility concepts through cooperative approaches.

I. M. Pires et al. (Eds.): GOODTECHS 2022, LNICST 476, pp. 19–36, 2023.
https://doi.org/10.1007/978-3-031-28813-5_2

(urban) area. In this context, a substantial part of air pollution is caused by the transportation sector [22].

One option to contribute to a reduction of air pollution in cities is to strengthen mobility-on-demand services [29] like ride-sharing in which multiple passengers share a vehicle or taxi. To decrease customers' waiting time and thereby increase the service's popularity, the number of requests at certain locations or the demand for taxis can be predicted; this prediction can be used to proactively reposition idle taxis to locations in which the demand exceeds the supply.

Predicting the demand for taxis is challenging as the temporal and spatial imbalance between demand and supply increases e.g. with a loss of experienced drivers due to demographic change [5,7]. Additionally, taxi drivers generally have a less efficient passenger search strategy in less known neighborhoods [5,7]. As the popularity of mobility-on-demand services like taxi ride-sharing increases [2,21,33], predicting the demand for taxis becomes even more relevant.

Usually, the demand is predicted for a short term like the next 30 min based on the previous demand, for instance in the last two hours. Many approaches train neural networks based on historic datasets with millions of taxi trips. Typically, the area of a city is spatially separated into multiple non-overlapping areas – like a 1000 m square grid cell – and the number of trips in each of these areas is predicted for the next time step. The grid cell size is understood as the edge length of the cell, e.g. a 1000 m sized square grid cell corresponds to an area of 1 km^2.

In Sect. 2, we present related work about taxi demand prediction to show that while using square/rectangular grids to spatially structure the demand is common, the chosen grid cell sizes vary from 150 m to 4900 m. In Sect. 3, we present the methodology for studying the influence of the chosen grid cell size on the prediction accuracy of multiple demand prediction approaches. The experimental results are presented in Sect. 4 and discussed in Sect. 5. Finally, a conclusion is given in Sect. 6.

2   Related Work

In recent years, researchers have made numerous advances in the field of taxi demand prediction [34]. Various approaches have been developed, which use, e.g., statistical time series analysis or making forecasts about the future by analyzing traffic data and using neural networks. As shown by [24] and in Table 1, while the commonly used evaluation metrics – Root Mean Square Error (RMSE), Mean Absolute Error (MAE), Mean Absolute Percentage Error (MAPE), or Mean Relative Error (MRE) – are obvious, there is a wider variation of the chosen network types. The most common network types are Convolutional Neural Network (CNN), Long Short-Term Memory Network (LSTM), and Graph Convolutional Neural Network (GCN). In the following, we describe related work on short-term taxi demand prediction for each of these three network types.

2.1   Convolutional Neural Networks

CNN models are mainly used in image and speech recognition. As taxi demand data organized by a square grid has a structure similar to an image [36], CNNs

Table 1. Overview of grid configurations of existing demand prediction approaches.

Reference	Grid topology	Cell size in meter	Evaluation metric	Basic method	Code
Chu, Lam, and Li [4]	Rectangualr	220×170	RMSE, SMAPE	LSTM & CNN	✗
Davis, Raina, and Jagannathan [5]	Rectangular	$1200\times 600, 4900\times 4900$	RMSE, SMAPE, MASE	LSTM	✗
Jin et al. [8]	Rectangular	$560\times 475^{\dagger}$	RMSE, MAE	GCN	✗
Ke et al. [9]	Polygons	N/A	RMSE, MAPE, MAE	GCN	✗
Ke et al. [10]	Polygons	N/A	RMSE, MAPE, MAE	GCN	✗
Ke et al. [11]	Square	4770×4810	RMSE, MAE, R-squared	LSTM & CNN	✗
Lee et al. [13]	Square	700×700	RMSE, MAPE	GCN	✗
Li and Axhausen [14]	Square	500×500	RMSE, SMAPE	GCN	✗
Oda and Joe-Wong [16]	Square	150×150	RMSE	CNN	✗
Pian and Wu [17]	Square	1000×1000	RMSE, MAPE, MAE	GCN	✓
Wang et al. [26]	Rectangular	2650×2600	RMSE, SMAPE	CNN	✓
Wu, Zhu, and Chen [27]	Square	700×700	RMSE, MAPE	GCN	✗
Xu and Li [30]	Square	300×300	RMSE, MAE, R-squared	GCN	✗
Xu et al. [28]	Square	153×153	RMSE, SMAPE	LSTM	✗
Yao et al. [31]	Square	700×700	RMSE, MAPE	LSTM & CNN	✓
Ye et al. [32]	Rectangular	720×420	RMSE, PCC	LSTM & CNN	✗
Zhang et al. [34]	Rectangular	$890 \times 910^{\dagger}$	RMSE, MAPE, MAE	RNN	✓
Zhang et al. [35]	Rectangular	$250 \times 334^{\dagger}$	RMSE, MAE	LSTM	✓
Zhang, Liu, and Zheng [37]	Square	1600×1600	RMSE, MAPE, MAE	CNN	✗

(S)MAPE: (Symmetric) Mean Absolute Percentage Error, MA(S)E: Mean Absolute (Scaled) Error, PCC: Pearson Correlation Coefficient, RMSE: Root Mean Square Error, N/A: Not Available
†Estimated based on coordinates

are also commonly used for taxi demand prediction due to their ability to identify spatial correlations [32].

Many authors use CNNs as demand prediction models or as building blocks for their network, such as [16,25,31,32,37]. As shown in Table 1, all CNN-based approaches use a square or rectangular grid topology, but the chosen grid cell size varies from 700 m in [31] to 1600 m in [25]. Interestingly, for most approaches CNN layers are the main building block – [16,25,37] – but some combine it with LSTM layers – [31,32]; the latter shows promising results for the prediction accuracy.

2.2 Recurrent Neural or Long Short-Term Memory Networks

While the usage of CNNs is often motivated by their ability to capture the spatial relation, Recurrent Neural Network (RNN)-based models are used to identify temporal relations in the training data [11,28,34]. While both CNNs and RNNs are able to process a sequence of input maps that represent the demand per grid cell and time step, RNNs process the input sequentially. In particular, they are able to save extracted information from previous inputs in their memory. As the classical RNN architecture suffers from the vanishing gradient problem [12], the architecture was enhanced to the Long Short-Term Memory Network architecture by Hochreiter and Schmidhuber [6]. As taxi demand prediction can be formalized as a sequence prediction problem, both RNNs and LSTM are suitable for this task [34].

Besides [31,32] that combine CNN and LSTM building blocks and were described above, [5,11,28,35] create an LSTM or an RNN – [34]. While all approaches use a square or rectangular grid, the chosen grid cell sizes vary from 153 m in [28] to 4900 m in [5]; three approaches – [31,32,34] – chose a grid cell size between 700 m and 900 m.

2.3   Graph Neural Networks

According to Li and Axhausen [14], CNN models have the limitation of using regular grids that compress the information, rather than irregularly shaped grids that may more closely approximate reality, e.g. the boroughs of a city; in contrast to CNNs, GCNs are able to handle such data. As taxi demand data are sometimes structured in irregularly shaped grids - like in the more recent records of the commonly used NYC Yellow Taxi Trip dataset [15] - and as shown in Table 1, GCNs are used to predict taxi demand. In graph neural networks the value predicted per node is computed over the values of its neighbour. GCNs represent spatial connections by non-euclidean graph structures and apply convolutional operations. The basic form of a GCN layer consists of graph convolution, a linear layer, and a nonlinear activation function [38]. While [9,10] make use of the graph networks' advantage by structuring the data with irregular polygons, [14] select a 500 m square grid. Surprisingly, all GCN-based approaches – [8,13,17,27,30] – do similar; the chosen grid cell sizes vary from 200 m to 1000 m.

2.4   Research Gap, Question, and Hypothesis

While many researchers use deep learning-based methods to predict the demand, the used grid cell sizes vary from 150 m in [16] to 4900 m in [5]; these variations also differ among the different neural network types commonly used. Surprisingly, only two approaches – [3,30] – consider the grid cell size as an optimizable parameter and optimize it: Chiang, Hoang, and Lim [3] compared grid cell sizes from 250 m to 4000 m and selected 250 m as it achieved the highest prediction accuracy measured via the metric perplexity. Xu and Li [30] compare grid cell sizes from 100 m to 400 m and select 300 m because the RMSE is the lowest.

Comparing the prediction accuracy measured on different grid cell sizes does not work per default; in Sect. 3.2 and Fig. 2 we illustrate this problem and propose an aggregation step to enable comparability. Neither [3] nor [30] describe such a step. Consequently, we assume that their methodology for choosing a grid cell size was not complete.

A change in the grid cell size affects (1) the average number of trips per cell, (2) the number of cells in which no trip occurs at a certain time step, as well as (3) the ability of a demand prediction model to capture spatial demand patterns in a city. Because of this, the high variability of grid cell sizes used by others, and the lack of a methodologically complete comparison as regards their influence, we consider the influence of grid cell sizes on the accuracy of demand prediction models as an open research gap.

This gap leads us to the following research question: **How does the grid cell size affects the accuracy of various neural network types for taxi demand prediction measured via MAE, MRE, and RMSE?**

In the context of this study, we restrict ourselves to the grid cell sizes of 250, 500 and 1000 m, as these are representative of the grid cell sizes used in the literature.

Smaller grid cell sizes might enable a demand prediction model to better capture the spatial patterns of a city; while a larger grid cell size might be sufficient to separate the demand patterns between city districts, a finer grid cell size could allow the separation of demand patterns in neighborhoods. Consequently, we select the hypothesis **H1: Smaller grid cell sizes achieve a higher prediction accuracy** to address the aforementioned research question.

3   Methodology

Here, we describe the dataset used in our experiment, as well as the evaluation metrics and aggregation step that enables a fair comparison of the results achieved on different grid cell sizes. Furthermore, we select five demand prediction approaches from the related work of the previous section and three baseline models. For each of the five selected models, we select the optimal grid cell size via measuring the prediction accuracy on the validation data. The final results are measured on the previously unseen test data. The parameters of each model were chosen with respect to the configurations of the authors of the respective model. Therefore, no optimization of the hyperparameters was performed. In general, the batch size is set to 256 and the demand is predicted for the next 30 min. Additionally, all external factors, such as weather information, were excluded from the prediction to allow for a consistent comparability of the grid cell configurations.

3.1   Dataset

We use the *NYC Yellow Taxi Trip Data* [15], which was created by the New York City Taxi & Limousine Commission. It is one of the most widely used datasets in the field of taxi demand prediction. We consider 18 months, starting from January 2015 and until June 2016. Almost 70% – about 12 months – of the data will be used for training the networks, about 20% – about 4 months – for validation, and the remaining 10% – about 2 months – for testing. To prepare the data and exclude outliers, we apply the same strategy as S. Schleibaum, J. P. Müller, and M. Sester [19]; that results in about 3.5% as outliers. In particular, we enhance the trip records by the indices of the grids with a cell size of 250, 500, and 1000 m. We select a square with the bottom left (40.5879, −74.0898) and the top right (40.9014, −73.6857) as the area in which the trips have to start. Figure 1 shows the absolute taxi demand in the area via a grid cell size of 250 m, which is equal to an area of $0.0625\,\mathrm{m}^2$.

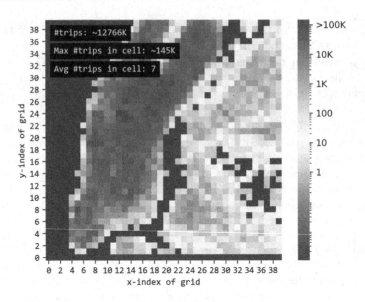

Fig. 1. Absolute number of taxi trips in New York City between January 2015 to June 2016 shown on a grid with cells size of 250 m and on a logarithmic scale

3.2 Evaluation

Metrics. To evaluate the performance, we use the three evaluation metrics commonly used: the MAE, MRE, and RMSE. In this approach y is used as the actual value, $\hat{y}$ as the predicted value, and N is the total number of values in the range of $n = 0, \ldots, N - 1$. The evaluation metrics are defined as follows: MAE as $\frac{1}{N} \sum_{n=1}^{N} |y_n - \hat{y}_n|$, MRE as $\frac{1}{N} \sum_{n=1}^{N} \frac{|y_n - \hat{y}_n|}{\hat{y}_n}$, and RMSE as $\sqrt{\frac{1}{N} \sum_{n=1}^{N} (y_n - \hat{y}_n)^2}$.

Illustration of the Comparability Problem. As shown in Fig. 2 the grid on the left and the grid in the middle are considered as two separate predictions. For example, comparing the prediction accuracy of the two cells with the MAE – $MAE_{1000\,m}^{NoAgg.}$ of 50 and $MAE_{500\,m}^{NoAgg.}$ of 12.5 – we see that the prediction accuracy is higher for a grid cell size of 500 m. However, that is incorrect because both, the true demand of one cell and the total predicted demand of all cells, are the same in both predictions. Consequently, predictions made on different grid cell sizes are not comparable by default.

Aggregation Step. To make the results on the two grid cell sizes comparable, we aggregate the four 500 m grid cells to the right grid cell in Fig. 2 by computing the two sums $\sum_{n=0}^{3} y_n$ and $\sum_{n=0}^{3} \hat{y}_n$. Now, comparing MAE – $MAE_{1000\,m}^{NoAgg.}$ of 50 and $MAE_{1000\,m}^{Agg.}$ of 50 – we see that the prediction accuracy is the same for the 1000 m sized grid cell and for the aggregated 1000 m sized grid cell.

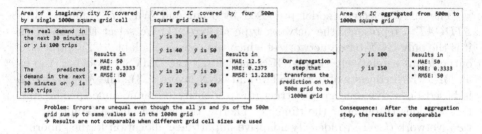

Fig. 2. Illustration of problem when comparing results from different grid cell sizes and our aggregation step to tackle this problem

Consequently, we aggregate the grid cells that occupy the same space as the largest grid cell size based on the geographical location of the grid cells. Technically, we apply two-dimensional average pooling and multiply the results by the number of cells aggregated, allowing the predicted value of a grid cell to be compared with the reference grid cell of size 1000 m.

3.3   Selection of Demand Prediction Approaches

The criteria for selecting demand prediction approaches from the related work are (C1) that we have at least one model per common network type – CNN, RNN, and GCN (C2) the availability of the source code so that we are able to reproduce the approach, and (C3) the prediction accuracy reported by the authors.

In Table 1, we list only one RNN-based model - corresponds to (C1) - proposed by Zhang et al. [34] and henceforth called *M1-MLRNN*. As the source code is available (C2) and the model outperformed simple LSTM models as well as ConvLSTM [20] and St-ResNet [36] (C3), we select this model. The authors first build a Spearman Correlation Coefficient matrix from historical taxi demand data, and thereby derive several clusters of taxi zones using a deterministic annealing algorithm. Afterwards, several modules composed of RNN and Fully Connected (FC) layers are built – a global one and one per cluster. Per grid cell, the global and cluster-based predictions are averaged. Thereby the *M1-MLRNN* combines global predictions with the cluster ones to predict the overall demand for pickups in a city.

As shown in Table 1, we list three purely and four partialy LSTM-based models (C1). Still, there is only one purely LSTM-based model proposed by Zhang et al. [35] – referred to as *M2-pmlLSTM* – of which the source code is available (C2). The authors were able to outperform a model that combines CNN and LSTM layers (C3). In contrast to [34], temporal classification is used instead of spatial clustering. The corresponding classifier time-feature encoder consists of FC layers that map demand data to a time class. Additionally, the demand is enhanced by denoising and passed through an LSTM layer. Both outputs are fused via another LSTM and FC layer and combined to the final prediction. Interestingly, the pick-up and drop-off demand are predicted and used as input.

The third selected model proposed by Pian and Wu [17] – named *M3-STDGAT* – represents the network type GCN (C1). We select this model as it is the only GCN-based network of which the code is available (C2) and it also outperforms a relatively simple GCN model and the DMVST model of Yao et al. [31], which consists of both LSTM and CNN layers (C3). The *M3-STDGAT* is based on a dynamic graph structure to identify dynamic time-specific spatial relations throughout the timeline. Therby, the authors use a Graph Attention Network (GAT) to identify adaptive importance allocation for neighboring regions based on pair-wise calculated correlations. The *M3-STDGAT* is composed of a spatial and a temporal module as well as a prediction layer, which combines the output of the former two. The spatial module aims to capture spatial patterns and is composed of several GAT blocks. The temporal module is based on an LSTM to determine temporal patterns in the demand.

Table 1 shows that the fourth selected model – presented by Wang, Hou, and Barth [25] and henceforth called *M4-CNNFC* – is the only CNN-based model (C1) of which the source code is available (C2). With this relatively simple CNN-based model, the authors were able to outperform an LSTM-based model (C3). After each layer of the *M4-CNNFC*, a pooling layer is applied to compress the information. After the two CNN layers, a FC is used to incorporate additional weather information and generate the demand prediction.

Although we have already introduced a CNN-based model, we select a second CNN-based model, which is presented by Oda and Joe-Wong [16]. It consists solely of three CNN layers and in contrast to [25], no pooling layers are used (C1). Therefore, we could successfully reproduce the model (C2). Despite the simple design, very good results were achieved (C3). This model does not use any additional features.

3.4   Baseline Models

The decision tree-based approach XGBoost of Chen and Guestrin [1] – referred to as *M6-XGB* – is selected as the first baseline model. Here, different machine learning concepts are applied, such as ensemble learning and gradient boosting. Further, XGBoost was also used by [9,17,34] as a baseline model. Additionally, we use relatively simple regression models as baseline: *M7-Ridge* and *M8-Lasso*. Both were previously used as baselines for demand prediction models, for instance by [9,17,31].

4   Experimental Results

The results of the experiments of the five selected models are described below in ascending order of model numbering: *M1-MLRNN*, *M2-pmlLSTM*, *M3-STDGAT*, *M4-CNNFC*, and *M5-CNN*. An overview of the results described in this section is given in Table 2.

Table 2. Comparison of the results of the experiments with validation data.

Model	Grid size	MAE [#trips]	MRE	RMSE
M1-MLRNN-C4	1000 m	1.4054	0.2911	3.172
M1-MLRNN-C3	500 m	**1.2114**	**0.2529**	**2.6177**
M1-MLRNN-C3	250 m	1.2544	0.2616	2.6248
M1-MLRNN-C1	1000 m	**1.1827**	**0.2424**	**2.55**
	500 m	1.1905	0.2425	2.5726
	250 m	1.2428	0.2581	2.7089
M2-pmlLSTM	1000 m	**1.1891**	**0.2443**	**2.5978**
	500 m	1.1971	0.2446	2.5967
	250 m	1.2570	0.2566	2.7619
M3-STDGAT	1000 m	1.1907	0.2483	2.5492
	500 m	$N/A^{\dagger}$	$N/A^{\dagger}$	$N/A^{\dagger}$
	250 m	$N/A^{\dagger}$	$N/A^{\dagger}$	$N/A^{\dagger}$
M4-CNNFC	1000 m	1.3064	0.2705	2.8142
	500 m	**1.2942**	**0.2655**	**2.7404**
	250 m	1.3393	0.2761	2.8516
M5-CNN	1000 m	**1.2082**	**0.2484**	**2.678**
	500 m	1.2224	0.2552	2.7274
	250 m	1.3146	0.2705	2.9446

† Execution not possible

4.1 M1-MLRNN: Multi-level Recurrent Neural Network

To rebuild *M1-MLRNN*, we had to adapt the model to our dataset, which differs in size and cell configuration from the experiments conducted in [34]. As argued in the previous section, we exclude weather and time information initially used in the approach. As the number of clusters depends on the dataset, we reproduce the deterministic annealing approach used. The results per grid cell size and for up to 12 clusters are shown in Fig. 3.

Suprisingly, for all grid cell sizes the use of a single cluster or no clustering achieved the highest prediction accuracy. Overall, we notice a strong fluctuation of the achieved MRE values. In Fig. 4 the pick-up demand aggregated over all cells of cluster are shown for six clusters and grid cells of size 1000 m. While some clusters are clearly separable – e.g. 2 from 6 – others – e.g. 3 from 6 – are not. The non-uniform behaviour of a cluster over time may cause the model to learn a distorted assumption about the behaviour of all cells. A prediction specific to this cluster based on the supposed uniform behavior will lead to a less accurate prediction.

Clustering is an essential part of the approach of Zhang et al. [34], but we were not able to reproduce its effectiveness. Consequently, we consider both *M1-MLRNN* with and without clustering to determine the influence of the grid cell

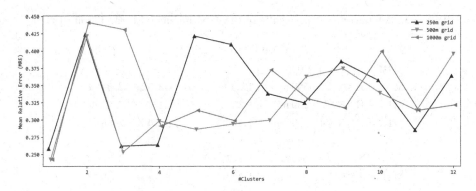

Fig. 3. *M1-MLRNN*: Selection of cluster size per grid cell size via MRE

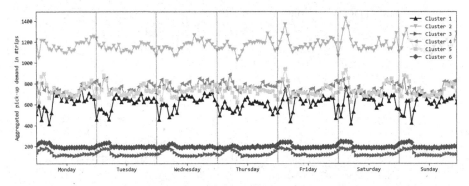

Fig. 4. Pick-up demand aggregated over a week for potential cluster sizes of the *M1-MLRNN* with a grid cell size of 1000 m

size on the *M1-MLRNN*. To distinguish between both configurations, we add the suffix -Cx, in which x represents the number of clusters used.

First, we study the results with the second-best number of clusters and secondly without clustering, which is equivalent to using exactly one cluster. Based on the results shown in Fig. 3, we choose the model configuration for the experiments with applied clustering to *M1-MLRNN-C4* in combination with 1000 m, and *M1-MLRNN-C3* with 500 m and 250 m. As shown in Table 2, for the applied clustering 500 m has the lowest MRE with a value of 0.2529 and the highest accuracy. In *M1-MLRNN-C1*, however, a different result is indicated. Here, the lowest MRE of 0.2529 is achieved with a grid cell size of 1000 m.

4.2 M2-pmlLSTM: Parallel Multi-task Learning Model

Also for the *M2-pmlLSTM* we had to do some adaptations before being able to run it on our dataset. This applies in particular to the time feature encoder. Additionally, as the model predicts both pick-up and drop-off demand, we adjusted the model to evaluate only the prediction accuracy of the pick-up demand. The experiments conducted with *M2-pmlLSTM* provide results similar to those of *M1-MLRNN-C1*. While the difference between the 250 m configuration and the 500 m/1000 m is relatively clear in all three evaluation metrics, the difference between the 500 m and 1000 m configuration is not. Even though the differences are small, we select the 1000 m grid cell size as the difference in the MAE is relatively large. With this configuration, the *M2-pmlLSTM* achieves an MAE of 1.1891, an MRE of 0.2443, and an RMSE of 2.5978 on the validation data.

4.3 M3-STDGAT: Spatial-Temporal Dynamic Graph Attention Network

The *M3-STDGAT* receives the previous demand of the last 2.5 h as a matrix and the corresponding adjacency matrix, which represents the connection between the grid cells. While the number of trainable parameters in GAT-based networks is independent of the input size, the incorporated RNN layer that increases this number significantly – from 6.6 M to 104.9 M parameters. For this reason, among others, we were unfortunately not able to conduct the experiments for *M3-STDGAT* completely. When using a 500 m grid instead of a 1000 m one, the total number of trainable parameters increases by 1393% leading to a required memory size of more than 64 GB. Additionally, the approximated time to calculate one training epoch is about 11 hours, if we use the grid cell size configuration of 500 m in a scaled-down version of the model. Therefore, a complete experiment would take more than 92 days. Consequently, we exclude the configuration of 500 m, and 250 m from the experiments. As shown in Table 2 the remaining results are an MAE of 1.2245, an MRE of 0.2492, and an RMSE of 2.7158.

4.4 M4-CNNFC: Convolutional Neural Network with Fully Connected Layer

To conduct the experiments with *M4-CNNFC* [26] we adjusted the network and, similar to the rebuilding of the other models, removed additional features. The results show that larger grid cells do not necessarily increase the prediction accuracy. As shown in Table 2, all evaluation metrics for the grid cell size of 500 m are smaller than for 1000 m, and 250 m – $MAE_{500\,m}$ of 1.2942, $MAE_{1000\,m}$ of 1.3064, and $MAE_{250\,m}$ of 1.3393.

4.5 M5-CNN: Convolutional Neural Network

In contrast to the results of the experiments of the *M4-CNNFC*, the *M5-CNN* achieves the highest prediction accuracy with a 1000 m grid cell size. As shown in Table 2, all error metrics are smaller for the cell size of 1000 m than for 500 m and 250 m – $MRE_{1000\,m}$ of 0.2484 vs. $MRE_{500\,m}$ of 0.2552 vs. $MRE_{250\,m}$ 0.2705.

5   Discussion

We will first discuss the RNN/LSTM-based models, followed by the CNN-based ones. Then the results of the RNN/LSTM and CNN-based models are discussed among each other. Finally, limitations are pointed out and interesting options for future work are proposed. However, due to the lack of experimental results for the grid cell sizes of 250 m and 500 m of *M3-STDGAT*, no discussion can be made for this model.

5.1   RNN-Based Models

As regards the *M1-MLRNN* derivatives from Zhang et al. [34], we achieve the highest prediction accuracy when *no* clustering is applied and a 1000 m grid cell size is used. If clustering is applied a grid cell size of 500 m achieves the highest prediction accuracy. It is worth noting that we were not able to reproduce the positive effect of clustering. As mentioned in Sect. 4.1, this is probably caused by the use of deterministic annealing as a clustering method, which seems to fail to perform sufficiently. It needs to be noted that deterministic annealing cannot guarantee to be able to find a minimum if more than one local minimum exists at a given temperature [18]. For this reason, deterministic annealing may not find the optimal clustering solution in our case.

In comparison, the experiments of *M2-pmlLSTM* show that the grid cell size of 1000 m leads to the highest prediction accuracy. This confirms that for RNN-based models, rather larger grid cell sizes are preferred over smaller ones.

In the side-by-side analysis of *M1-MLRNN* and *M2-pmlLSTM*, it can be found that the difference between the cell size of 1000 m, and 500 m is relatively small. Therefore, based on the results described neither for *M1-MLRNN* nor for *M2-pmlLSTM* is it possible to unambiguously answer the question of whether a large or a medium cell size provides the best result for RNN/LSTM-based models.

The results show that for both models hypothesis H1 – smaller grid cells allow for higher prediction accuracy – has to be rejected, as either the largest or a medium grid cell size is preferred.

5.2   CNN-Based Models

The results of the experiments of *M4-CNNFC* [26] show that the grid cell size configuration of 500 m is significantly better than for other grid cell sizes. In contrast, the largest size of the grid cell for *M5-CNN* [16] is considerably better. The two models, and thus the results, differ mostly in that *M4-CNNFC* [26] uses an FC prediction layer in addition to CNN layers; whereas, *M5-CNN* [16] consists of only three CNN layers. Therefore, when using only CNN layers, larger grid cell sizes should be selected.

Similar to the RNN-based models, the results for CNN-based models show that for both models, hypothesis H1 – smaller grid cells allow for higher prediction accuracy – has to be rejected, as the largest – *M5-CNN* – and medium – *M4-CNNFC* – grid cell size is preferred.

5.3   Comparison Among Models and to Baselines

The results from the experiments with testing data shown in Table 3 reveal that the results for *M1-MLRNN-C1*, *M2-pmlLSTM*, and *M3-STDGAT* are almost the same, as they all have the highest prediction accuracy by using the largest grid cell size. Furthermore, the results show that these three more complex models perform the best followed by *M1-MLRNN-C3*, *M5-CNN*, and *M4-CNNFC*. *M1-MLRNN-C3* and *M4-CNNFC* performed best when using the medium-sized grid cell size and *M5-CNN* when using the largest grid cell size.

When comparing these five models with the three baseline models, the advantage of deep learning-based models is apparent. The best result of the baseline models was obtained with *M7-Ridge* – MAE_{M7} of 1.2997 – followed by *M8-Lasso* and *M6-XGB* as shown in Table 3. If we compare the strongest baseline model *M7-Ridge* to the four models examined, we can see that *M7-Ridge* performs better than *M4-CNNFC* in only two of three metrics – MAE and MRE –, but also undercuts the MRE of *M1-MLRNN-C1* by 0.0029. Compared to *M1-MLRNN-C1*, however, the MAE is higher by 0.0399.

Although the considered models work differently depending on the grid cell configuration, our hypothesis H1 – smaller grid cells enable a higher prediction accuracy – needs to be rejected. Instead, the grid cell size should be considered individually for each model configuration. Especially since the results are partly close to each other, we assume that the influences of the individual components can strengthen or weaken each other. This is particularly important when different models are used as base models. Assumably, in the majority of papers, the grid cell size was chosen independently of the models. The results of this paper contradict this approach and indicate that a fair comparison between models is not possible if one grid cell size is chosen for all models, which could suppress good results for some models.

In addition, the grid cell size is often predefined based on the application. Therefore, it is recommended, according to our results, to choose a model that performs best for the specific grid cell size.

Another important aspect in comparing the models is the usage of pick-up and drop-off demand by *M1-MLRNN*, *M2-pmlLSTM*, and *M3-STDGAT*. Whereas *M4-CNNFC* and *M5-CNN* are based exclusively on the pick-up demand. Thus, the pick-up demand prediction is extended by the drop-off demand feature. In this work a consideration of the drop-off data as external features was not carried out, as the dropoff data is an essential part of the model structure. Nevertheless, we expect the drop-off data to influence the accuracy.

5.4   Limitations and Future Work

In this paper, we limited the comparison to three different grid cell configurations in terms of size – 1000 m, 500 m, and 250 m. However, the results of the experiments show that medium-sized and large-sized cells have a positive influence on the prediction accuracy of different models. Therefore, intermediate grid cell sizes between 500 m and 1000 m – such as 700 m following Wu, Zhu, and Chen

Table 3. Comparison of the models on the best grid cell size among each other and to the baseline models on the test data.

Model	Grid size	MAE [#trips]	MRE	RMSE
M1-MLRNN-C3	500 m	1.2598	0.2588	2.7588
M1-MLRNN-C1	1000 m	1.2341	0.2437	2.6990
M2-pmlLSTM	1000 m	1.2339	0.2433	2.6911
M3-STDGAT	1000 m	**1.2338**	**0.2410**	**2.6796**
M4-CNNFC	500 m	1.3416	0.2638	2.8367
M5-CNN	1000 m	1.2630	0.2486	2.8081
M6-XGB	1000 m[†]	1.5887	0.3128	3.1796
M7-Ridge	1000 m[†]	1.2997	0.2559	2.8400
M8-Lasso	1000 m[†]	1.4733	0.2901	3.1122

[†] Other configurations were not tested

[27], Lee et al. [13], and Yao et al. [31] – and grid cell sizes larger than 1000 m – for example 1500 m or 2500 m – similar to Zhang, Liu, and Zheng [37] and Wang et al. [26] – could be chosen.

Linked to the grid cell configuration, a limitation of our approach is that we do not consider the influence of the angle at which the grid cells are placed on the city map. Possibly, there is an influence on the prediction accuracy depending on the orientation of the grid cells relative to the orientation of the main roads of a city.

Furthermore, models with different combinations of layer types could be investigated. Thus, a pure FC network could be considered, as well as, combinations of CNN layers with LSTM layers, or different kinds of GCNs with LSTM layers.

Furthermore, as already described in Sect. 5.3, *M1-MLRNN*, *M2-pmlLSTM* and *M3-STDGAT* include both pick-up and drop-off demand in the calculation, whereas *M4-CNNFC* and *M5-CNN* – as well as *M6-XGB*, *M7-Ridge*, and *M8-Lasso* – only use the pick-up demand. The usage of drop-off demand can be considered as using an additional feature, like weather, population density, and points of interest. Therefore, the influence of these external factors on the accuracy of the prediction in combination with the size of the grid cell could also be investigated.

Another aspect is the usage of different datasets. Here, only the TLC dataset from New York City is used in the experiments, which limits the general explanatory value. Using a dataset from, for example, China – like [17,31,37] – could potentially affect the results, as there is a different traffic behavior and a different topology of the city. Here, it was difficult for us to get access a large taxi trip dataset from China.

6   Conclusion

When combining different network types in a model – e.g. CNN or LSTM layers in combination with FC layers – we could obtain different conclusions. According to our results, the grid cell size should be considered individually for each model configuration. This is especially important to consider when different models are used to evaluate the performance of new models. Therefore, we propose to consider the grid cell size as a tunable parameter in demand prediction models. Still, following our results a large grid cell size should be considered for a CNN model and a large or medium grid cell size should be selected for RNN or LSTM models.

However, depending on the use case of demand prediction, a smaller or medium-sized grid cell size might even be better – despite a slight decrease in accuracy – as, for example, the repositioning of taxis in ride-sharing can be done more precisely. In future approaches, a finer subdivision of the grid cell size, the influence of drop-off demand, as well as the influence of the angle of the dataset, could be investigated more closely to further improve prediction accuracy.

References

1. Chen, T., Guestrin, C.: XGBoost: a scalable tree boosting system. In: Proceedings of the 22nd ACM SIGKDD International Conference on Knowledge Discovery and Data Mining, KDD 2016, New York, NY, USA, pp. 785–794. Association for Computing Machinery (2016). https://doi.org/10.1145/2939672.2939785. ISBN 9781450342322
2. Chen, W., Chen, J., Yin, G.: Exploring side effects of ridesharing services in urban China: role of pollution - averting behavior. Electron. Commer. Res. **12**(4), 317 (2020). https://doi.org/10.1007/s10660-020-09443-y. ISSN 1389-5753
3. Chiang, M.-F., Hoang, T.-A., Lim, E.-P.: Where are the passengers? A grid-based gaussian mixture model for taxi bookings. In: Ali, M., Huang, Y., Gertz, M., Renz, M., Sankaranarayanan, J. (eds.) Proceedings of the 23rd SIGSPATIAL International Conference on Advances in Geographic Information Systems, New York, NY, USA, pp. 1–10. ACM (2015). https://doi.org/10.1145/2820783.2820807. ISBN 9781450339674
4. Chu, K.F., Lam, A.Y.S., Li, V.O.K.: Travel demand prediction using deep multiscale convolutional LSTM network. In: 2018 21st International Conference on Intelligent Transportation Systems (ITSC), pp. 1402–1407. IEEE (2018). https://doi.org/10.1109/ITSC.2018.8569427. ISBN 978-1-7281-0321-1
5. Davis, N., Raina, G., Jagannathan, K.: Grids versus graphs: partitioning space for improved taxi demand-supply forecasts. IEEE Trans. Intell. Transp. Syst. **22**(10), 6526–6535 (2021). https://doi.org/10.1109/TITS.2020.2993798
6. Hochreiter, S., Schmidhuber, J.: Long short-term memory. Neural Comput. **9**(8), 1735–1780 (1997). https://doi.org/10.1162/neco.1997.9.8.1735. ISSN 0899-7667
7. Ishiguro, S., Kawasaki, S., Fukazawa, Y.: Taxi demand forecast using real-time population generated from cellular networks. In: Proceedings of the 2018 ACM International Joint Conference and 2018 International Symposium on Pervasive and Ubiquitous Computing and Wearable Computers, New York, NY, USA, pp. 1024–1032. ACM (2018). https://doi.org/10.1145/3267305.3274157. ISBN 9781450359665

8. Jin, G., Xi, Z., Sha, H., Feng, Y., Huang, J.: Deep Multi-view spatiotemporal virtual graph neural network for significant citywide ride-hailing demand prediction. CoRR, abs/2007.15189 (2020)

9. Ke, J., Feng, S., Zhu, Z., Yang, H., Ye, J.: Joint predictions of multi-modal ride-hailing demands: a deep multi-task multi-graph learning-based approach. Transp. Rese. Part C Emerg. Technol. **127** (2021). https://doi.org/10.1016/j.trc.2021.103063. ISSN 0968-090X

10. Ke,' J., Qin, X., Yang, H., Zheng, Z., Zhu, Z., Ye, J.: Predicting origin-destination ride-sourcing demand with a spatio-temporal encoder-decoder residual multi-graph convolutional network (2019)

11. Ke, J., Zheng, H., Yang, H., Chen, X.M.: Short-term forecasting of passenger demand under on-demand ride services: a spatio-temporal deep learning approach. Transp. Res. Part C Emerg. Technol. **85**, 591–608 (2017). https://doi.org/10.1016/j.trc.2017.10.016. ISSN 0968-090X

12. Kolen, J.F., Kremer, S.C. (eds.) A Field Guide to Dynamical Recurrent Networks. IEEE (2009). https://doi.org/10.1109/9780470544037. ISBN 9780470544037

13. Lee, D., Jung, S., Cheon, Y., Kim, D., You, S.: Demand forecasting from spatiotemporal data with graph networks and temporal-guided embedding (2019)

14. Li, A., Axhausen, K.W.: Short-term traffic demand prediction using graph convolutional neural networks. AGILE GISci. Ser. **1**, 1–14 (2020). https://doi.org/10.5194/agile-giss-1-12-2020

15. NYC Taxi and Limousine Commission. TLC Trip Record Data. https://www1.nyc.gov/site/tlc/about/tlc-trip-record-data.page

16. Oda, T., Joe-Wong, C.: MOVI: a model-free approach to dynamic fleet management. In: IEEE INFOCOM 2018 - IEEE Conference on Computer Communications, pp. 2708–2716 (2018). https://doi.org/10.1109/INFOCOM.2018.8485988

17. Pian, W., Wu, Y.: Spatial-temporal dynamic graph attention networks for ride-hailing demand prediction (2020)

18. Rose, K.: Deterministic annealing for clustering, compression, classification, regression, and related optimization problems. Proc. IEEE **86**(11), 2210–2239 (1998). https://doi.org/10.1109/5.726788

19. Schleibaum, S., Müller, J.P., Sester, M.: Enhancing expressiveness of models for static route-free estimation of time of arrival in urban environments. Transp. Res. Proc. **62**, 432–441 (2022). https://doi.org/10.1016/j.trpro.2022.02.054, https://www.sciencedirect.com/science/article/pii/S2352146522001818. ISSN 2352-1465, 24th Euro Working Group on Transportation Meeting

20. Shi, X., Chen, Z., Wang, H., Yeung, D.-Y., Wong, W., Woo, W.: Convolutional LSTM network: a machine learning approach for precipitation nowcasting. In: Proceedings of the 28th International Conference on Neural Information Processing Systems, NIPS 2015, Cambridge, MA, USA, vol. 1, pp. 802–810. MIT Press (2015). https://dl.acm.org/doi/10.5555/2969239.2969329

21. Uber Technologies Inc., Financials (2021). https://investor.uber.com/financials/default.aspx

22. United Nations. Sustainable Transport, Sustainable Development. Interagency Report for Second Global Sustainable Transport Conference (2021). https://sdgs.un.org/publications/interagency-report-second-global-sustainable-transport-conference

23. United Nations. Billions of people still breathe unhealthy air: new WHO data (2022). https://www.who.int/news/item/04-04-2022-billions-of-people-still-breathe-unhealthy-air-new-who-data/

24. Varghese, V., Chikaraishi, M., Urata, J.: Deep learning in transport studies: a meta-analysis on the prediction accuracy. J. Big Data Anal. Transp. **2**(3), 199–220 (2020). https://doi.org/10.1007/s42421-020-00030-z. ISSN 2523-3556

25. Wang, C., Hou, Y., Barth, M.: Data-driven multi-step demand prediction for ride-hailing services using convolutional neural network. Adv. Comput. Vision 11–22 (2019). . https://doi.org/10.1007/978-3-030-17798-0_2, https://dx.doi.org/10.1007/978-3-030-17798-0_2. ISSN 2194-5365

26. Wang, Y., Yin, H., Chen, H., Wo, T., Xu, J., Zheng, K.: Origin-destination matrix prediction via graph convolution: a new perspective of passenger demand modeling. In: Teredesai, A., Kumar, V., Li, Y., Rosales, R., Terzi, E., Karypis, G. (eds.) Proceedings of the 25th ACM SIGKDD International Conference on Knowledge Discovery & Data Mining, New York, NY, USA, pp. 1227–1235. ACM (2019). https://doi.org/10.1145/3292500.3330877. ISBN 9781450362016

27. Wu, M., Zhu, C., Chen, L.: Multi-task spatial-temporal graph attention network for taxi demand prediction. In: Proceedings of the 2020 5th International Conference on Mathematics and Artificial Intelligence, New York, NY, USA, pp. 224–228. ACM (2010). https://doi.org/10.1145/3395260.3395266. ISBN 9781450377072

28. Xu, J., Rahmatizadeh, R., Boloni, L., Turgut, D.: Real-time prediction of taxi demand using recurrent neural networks. IEEE Trans. Intell. Transp. Syst. **19**(8), 2572–2581 (2018). https://doi.org/10.1109/TITS.2017.2755684. ISSN 1524-9050

29. Xu, Y., Li, D.: Incorporating graph attention and recurrent architectures for city-wide taxi demand prediction. ISPRS Int. J. Geo-Inf. **8**(9) (2019). https://doi.org/10.3390/ijgi8090414, https://www.mdpi.com/2220-9964/8/9/414. ISSN 2220-9964

30. Ying, X., Li, D.: Incorporating graph attention and recurrent architectures for city-wide taxi demand prediction. ISPRS Int. J. Geo Inf. **8**(9), 414 (2019). https://doi.org/10.3390/ijgi8090414

31. Yao, H., et al.: Deep multi-view spatial-temporal network for taxi demand prediction. In: 32nd AAAI Conference on Artificial Intelligence, AAAI 2018, pp. 2588–2595. AAAI Press (2018). https://doi.org/10.1609/aaai.v32i1.11836

32. Ye, J., Sun, L., Du, B., Fu, Y., Tong, X., Xiong, H.: Co-prediction of multiple transportation demands based on deep spatio-temporal neural network. In: Teredesai, A., Kumar, V., Li, Y., Rosales, R., Terzi, E., Karypis, G. (eds.) Proceedings of the 25th ACM SIGKDD International Conference on Knowledge Discovery & Data Mining, New York, NY, USA, pp. 305–313. ACM (2019). https://doi.org/10.1145/3292500.3330887. ISBN 9781450362016

33. Zardini, G., Lanzetti, N., Pavone, M., Frazzoli, E.: Analysis and control of autonomous mobility-on-demand systems. Annu. Rev. Control Robot. Auton. Syst. **5**(1) (2022). https://doi.org/10.1146/annurev-control-042920-012811

34. Zhang, C., Zhu, F., Lv, Y., Ye, P., Wang, F.-Y.: MLRNN: taxi demand prediction based on multi-level deep learning and regional heterogeneity analysis. IEEE Trans. Intell. Transp. Syst. 1–11 (2021). https://doi.org/10.1109/TITS.2021.3080511. ISSN 1524-9050

35. Zhang, C., Zhu, F., Wang, X., Sun, L., Tang, H., Lv, Y.: Taxi demand prediction using parallel multi-task learning model. IEEE Trans. Intell. Transp. Syst. 1–10 (2020). https://doi.org/10.1109/TITS.2020.3015542. ISSN 1524-9050

36. Zhang, J., Zheng, Y., Qi, D.: Deep spatio-temporal residual networks for citywide crowd flows prediction. In: Proceedings of the Thirty-First AAAI Conference on Artificial Intelligence, AAAI 2017, pp. 1655–1661. AAAI Press (2017). https://doi.org/10.5555/3298239.3298479

37. Zhang, K., Liu, Z., Zheng, L.: Short-term prediction of passenger demand in multi-zone level: temporal convolutional neural network with multi-task learning. IEEE Trans. Intell. Transp. Syst. **21**(4), 1480–1490 (2020). https://doi.org/10.1109/TITS.2019.2909571. ISSN 1524-9050

38. Zhou, J., et al.: Graph neural networks: a review of methods and applications. AI Open **1**, 57–81 (2020). https://doi.org/10.1016/j.aiopen.2021.01.001, https://www.sciencedirect.com/science/article/pii/S2666651021000012. ISSN 2666-6510

Social

Parents as Active Agents in Building Emotionally Stable, and Healthy Communities: Testing PSsmile App

Teresa Maria Sgaramella[1(✉)], Lea Ferrari[1], Vida Drasutè[2,3], Margherita Bortoluzzi[1], and Stefano Corradi[2,3]

[1] University of Padova, Padova, Italy
teresamaria.sgaramella@unipd.it
[2] Kaunas University of Technology, Kaunas, Lithuania
[3] e-Mundus, Kaunas, Lithuania

Abstract. There is an increasing interest in implementing innovative actions tailored to Social and Emotional Learning (SEL) in children. Higher SEL is linked to successful participation in school life, better health, positive youth development. Moreover, research show that to pursue these goals, it is mandatory that adults acquire and apply knowledge, skills, and attitudes enhancing Social and Emotional Competences. ICTs applications should align with this perspectives' taking and involve significant adults in the educational settings. The paper fully describes the Mobile application PSsmile developed as intellectual output of the Erasmus+ PSsmile project, the recent steps undertaken to support effective use of this app. It is aimed at raising parents and teachers' awareness, promoting and strengthening their personal Social-Emotional competences making them more effective agents of the positive growth for children and for their communities.

Keywords: Social and Emotional Competences · Parents · PSsmile mobile app

1 Introduction

Social and Emotional Learning is an integral part of human education and development and is the process through which everyone, children, and adults develop the skills, attitudes, and values necessary to acquire social and emotional competence. Social-emotional competence refers to "the ability to use social and emotional skills and knowledge to be resourceful, adapt to, respect, and work well with others, and take personal and collective responsibility" [1].

Within the most well-known model of SEL, these skills are organized as five interacting components: self-awareness (the ability to understand one's own emotions, personal

PSsmile project has been co-funded by the European Commission through the Erasmus+ Programme. This paper reflects the views only of the authors, and the Commission cannot be held responsible for any use which may be made of the information contained therein.

I. M. Pires et al. (Eds.): GOODTECHS 2022, LNICST 476, pp. 39–53, 2023.
https://doi.org/10.1007/978-3-031-28813-5_3

goals, and values); self-management (the ability to regulate affects and calm oneself down); social awareness (the ability to understand others and take the perspective of those with different backgrounds and cultures, and to act with empathy and compassion); relationship skills (the ability to communicate clearly, to negotiate and to seek help, when needed) and the ability to take responsible decisions [2, 3].

Social and Emotional Education (SEE) refers to the educational process by which an individual develops social and emotional competence for personal, social, and academic growth and development through curricular, embedded, relational and contextual approaches [4]. Supporting SEL development increases, in fact, the chance of academic and workplace success reduces emotional distress and risks of behavioral problems, improvement of participation in the school context [5].

1.1 Supporting the Development of Key Social and Emotional Competence

The development of core competences depends on the quality of relationships that a child has the possibility to experience in different settings, including their families, schools, and communities [6]. Emerging evidence suggests that the recent pandemic may have exacerbated existing inequalities and created new inequalities. Students who are disadvantaged—including children from poor families, girls, children with disabilities, and those living in rural and disadvantaged regions—may have faced the biggest challenges both in terms of continuing their learning and of maintaining social and emotional contact [7]. As teachers underline, to this still active challenge new challenges are added for children as well as for adults, that is threats to peaceful life in diverse world contexts.

Social-emotional competence programs conducted in schools have been shown to be effective in promoting positive, behavioral, and academic results that are important for healthy development; predicting important results related to the future; support the behavior change process [8].

School-based programs are effective in preventing school violence, including bullying [9, 10]. Schools can be seen then as an ideal place to provide learning activities designed to help future adults achieve their best leadership chances, happy, healthy, and independent lives, and reach their unique career potential.

2 Opening Social-Emotional Learning to the Educational Community

Fostering SEL requires implementing practices and policies that help not only students but also adults acquire and apply knowledge, skills, and attitudes that enhance personal development, social relationships, and effective, productive work thus impacting the quality of life, satisfaction, and participation in diverse contexts of adults' life [11–13].

SEL development for teachers to support high-quality instruction is considered fundamental for the school of the future: higher SEL competences benefit class management and students' school and personal development [14]. As concern parents, evidence exists that positive parenting roles and SEL practices support children's efforts in school and lead to academic achievement and social skills improvement [15, 16]. Moreover, an effective school-family partnership is effective in supporting and four improving children's learning. Additionally, benefits for children, teachers and families are achieved through positive changes in social skills and adaptive children's behaviors [17].

Parents represent the first socialization agency that shapes their children's social and emotional development and the benefit of growing up in a family environment permeated by SEL is translated into a positive parent-child relationship [18, 19]. Children that experience a socially and emotionally supportive environment are more likely to develop positive relationships both with teachers and peers [20] as well as better school motivation, engagement, and better grades [21].

Moreover, with their parenting and as role models the parents' social and emotional skills can help children to negotiate the numerous challenges and inequalities they experience in school and social contexts such as socioeconomic status, gender stereotypes, and ethnic prejudices thus significantly contributing to mental health and well-being [22].

Finally, involving parents and establishing a positive school-family partnership has been recognized as one of the drivers that can make a difference in achieving successful children's development.

2.1 Building Social and Emotional Competencies in the Educational Community

The premise for the proposal presented in this work is The European project PSsmile (Social-Emotional Capacity Building in Primary Education, http://smile.emundus.lt/). Beginning in 2019, it involves teams from Bulgaria, Greece, Italy, Lithuania, and Portugal. This project has its pillars in Social Emotional Education as a capacity-building process that involves all children, especially those from low-income, underrepresented backgrounds, and high-risk populations.

Based on the Positive Youth Development approach [23] the project develops along key goals. The first aim is in developing a training program for primary school teachers; the second one is to develop a training program for children to promote their SE skills to make them more ready to think about their future and facilitate school transitions. A third aim, specifically relevant to this work, is to provide teachers and parents with a tool aimed at fostering their SE skills, which is a specific app.

Following recent theoretical studies and challenges to everyone's well-being, promoting social-emotional competence in our view requires methodological choices and actions:

- Consider both emotional and social dimensions. It is mandatory to encourage and reinforce social skills such as greeting others, taking turns, cooperation and resolving conflicts, devoting a specific space to emotions and behaviors, knowledge and action level, awareness, and management skills.
- Adopt a 'double lenses approach.' Looking at the present and future objectives and undertaking a positive approach supports the decision-making process in all proposed activities.
- Actively, and personally involve significant adults. Creating an environment where adults take care of their Social and Emotional Well-being and children feel safe to

express their emotions with the contribution of teachers and family is essential for healthy social-emotional outcomes [24].

– Adopt innovative and at the same time easy-to-access technologies. Information and Communication Technologies can support Social-Emotional Competencies (SECs) development by providing innovative tools (see, videogames and mobile apps) designed to teach self-management exercises [25] and delivering fast and easily accessible courses and materials [26, 27].

These choices guide both the curricula developed for children and the educational activities proposed to the meaningful adults in their life.

3   The PSsmile App: An Integrative Tool for a Community-Based Education

PSsmile Mobile App is an intellectual output of the Erasmus + project "Social-emotional Capacity Building in Primary Education" (PSsmile). PSsmile aims to foster the development of socio-emotional capacity in primary education institutions by engaging in its activities with the whole community.

The PSsmile mobile app falls within this wider project goal, as it aims to develop a greater awareness of socio-emotional intelligence and deeper control of its related skills. The app can be seen as an opportunity to apply the most relevant outcomes within SEL studies, portraying a viable solution for those problems that have been often indicated in SEL curricula.

By raising adults' awareness of SEL's importance and developing their social-emotional competences, the app contributes to building emotionally stable, inclusive, and healthy communities where they take care of their own social-emotional functioning and support its development in children.

3.1   Drivers of the App

The app includes many daily exercises, a thorough and accurate explanation of the background knowledge on which SEL is based, infographics showing the progress made by the users, and a questionnaire for feedback, providing relevant data for research and the opportunity to improve the app, making it more suitable for the users. This organization escorts the learners through the entire course, building participants' social-emotional skills in an incremental way, one that adapts itself to the needs of the trainee.

Parents and teachers have their own dedicated sections and activities since they play different and specific roles in children's social-emotional development. Additionally, the PSsmile app is unique because it can also be used by parents and teachers simultaneously, making them active agents of change supporting positive development in future adults [28].

3.2 The Five-Week Program and Its Content

The *PSsmile Mobile App*, as shown in a recent paper [29] includes activities developing on a five-week-long programme (Fig. 1).

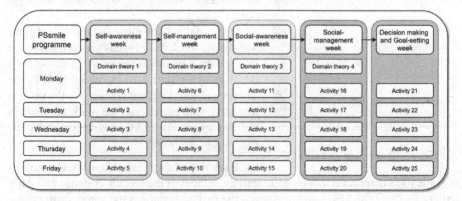

Fig. 1. PSsmile programme structure

The first four weeks are dedicated to getting acquainted with all the SEL domains, namely (i) Self-awareness, (ii) Self-management, (iii) Social-awareness, and (iv) Social-management, respectively. The fifth week is dedicated to learning to take responsible decisions and thinking about the future.

3.3 The Structure

The first thing a new user sees after logging in is a page containing the rules of the five-week *PSsmile Mobile App* and here user can get acquainted with the SEL domains by reading more about them (Fig. 2).

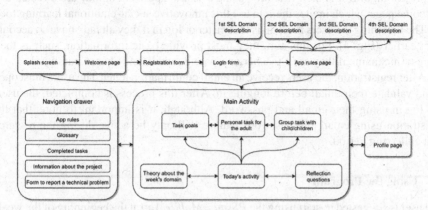

Fig. 2. Individual components of the programme

Fig. 3. Sign in page and menu

After agreeing to the programme rules, the users are presented with the Main activity. Main Activity has a bottom navigation bar connecting it to the Theory and *Reflection Questions* sections, as well as a *Profile* page button at the top right corner (Fig. 3).

If they did not download the app at the beginning of the week (on Monday), a notification on this screen will invite the users to come back on Monday or start learning about SEL in the Theory section. The best practice for the users is always to read more about the week's domain in the Theory section on Monday, before doing the first task of the week.

Each day of the week, from Monday to Friday, this page displays a unique SEL activity, related to the week's domain. The daily activity section is divided into three tabs – the first one contains the name, instructions, and goals of the daily task, usually paired with a visual; the second one contains a detailed description of the task that the adult must do alone, and the third one contains a detailed description of the task the adult must complete with a child or children.

To score points, the user must click the completion-confirming buttons in the second and third tabs and answer all three reflection questions.

For the users' convenience, the *Main Activity* also contains a navigation drawer in the top left corner. Here the user finds the rules of the five-week program, a glossary with more complex definitions presented in the content, a section to review already completed tasks, a section to read more about the *PSsmile* project, as well as a form to report a technical problem.

The application is implemented using Android Studio. When users open the application, they are always greeted with a Splash screen – a colorful loading screen containing the project logo. If it is their first time using *PSsmile* application, they are directed to a Welcome page, which invites them to use this innovative social-emotional learning tool.

The first thing the users must do is to register or log in if they already have an account from earlier (Fig. 4). For this aim, they must provide basic information, such as their name or nickname if they are a teacher or a parent, email, and chosen password.

After registration, the users receive an email confirmation letter. The users must open it and validate their email before logging in. After this process is completed, the users can log in using their email and password. Although, it is important to note, that the registration using email and password feature will only be active during the research data collecting period.

3.4 Using the Program

The user is suggested to start using the *PSsmile Mobile App* at the beginning of the week. Every Monday morning the user should read the theory to learn more about the week's domain. In addition, each working day the user should read the first part of the daily task in the morning. After that, during the day, at any convenient time the adult should mindfully do the personal task, and only after that experience the task with a child or children. It is evident that adult should first learn more about SEL skills and evaluate them on themselves before practice with children.

Weekends are meant for resting or if one wishes – reading more about SEL, repeating activities.

3.5 A Closer Look to the App: Starting the Activities

Fig. 4. Screenshots from day one

When the users start to use the *PSsmile Mobile App*, they will first encounter a description of the first domain – Self-Awareness – and then the first activity titled the Tree of emotions (Fig. 4). With this task, the users start their social and emotional learning journey by improving how to better express emotions verbally.

3.6 Data Collection and Participant Profile

Basic information (name or nickname, gender, and age group) is collected from each participant: Status (parent or teacher), Activities completed, Domain and Final score, Answers to *Reflection Questions* the participant answers after each activity, and Answers to the App Evaluation Questionnaire.

The reflective questions represent an important section for users to self-monitoring their learning across the five domains. They could increase their awareness of domains where they experienced more difficulties or reached higher goals, where they gained more benefits in everyday life. This section also provides useful information on the activities that have an impact on the users, and which ones were disregarded. For the same reason, the tool includes the App Evaluation Questionnaire with the following questions:

The program I participated in was unique and positively different from other experiences I have had.

Information was presented in a straightforward way.

Interacting with the app was simple.

The navigation structure was easy to use.

The application interface was visually appealing.

Do you have any suggestions for the creators?

Respondents are required to provide an answer using a Likert scale ranging from 1 (Strongly disagree) to 5 (Strongly agree).

4   PSsmile App's Modules

The modules developed within PSsmile mobile app are based on the five domains defined within the Methodological Guide developed through the cooperative effort of all project partners. The modules are:

Self-awareness: This refers to the users' ability to describe their own emotions; to understand why they feel the way they do (Yoder, 2014). This module also aims to develop an accurate understanding of themselves, focusing both on individual strengths and deficiencies, to identify areas that need improvement.

Self-management. This domain often includes meta-cognitive skills, which go from being able to cope with stress and manage emotions to developing positive motivation and a sense of hope and optimism. Self-management skills play a significant role in dramatically reducing the risks of emotional problems, attention deficit, internalizing and externalizing disorders, as well as decreasing the uptake of unhealthy habits (Shanker 2014).

Social Awareness. Within this domain, users will improve their ability to take others' perspectives into account and they will also increase their empathy, learning how to recognize the emotions of others and manage their own according to the social contexts. Particularly important in this regard is also the ability to recognize and appreciate diversity.

Social Management. Also called *"Relationship Skills"* in the CASEL Framework (CASEL, 2020), it includes the skills useful for establishing and maintaining healthy and supportive relationships. People with important levels of *social management* can navigate settings with diverse individuals and groups by communicating clearly, listening actively, cooperating, and working in group to solve problems.

Decision Making and Future Goals Setting. Decision making refers to the ability to develop appropriate strategies to solve problems, whether academic, personal, or social. This competence includes strong personal and prosocial dimensions, as people acquiring it need to become more self-reflective and learn how to make decisions based on moral, personal, and ethical standards, recognizing the importance of making responsible decisions that affect themselves and others. As Fig. 5 shows, they represent the overarching component within the *"PSmile Framework"*, as both participate in the development of awareness and management.

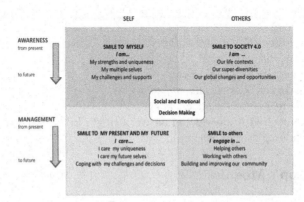

Fig. 5. Visual representation of the domains and the overarching components in PSsmile project

Activities are not immediately available to users, but they are unlocked after 24 h. This is expected to promote incremental skills development and to provide learners with enough time to reflect on what they have learned.

Each day is further divided in two sections:

Theory and Tasks. The first provides an overview of the domain's theme, illustrating to the user the theoretical background of the activities and the skills they will learn. The second, instead, provides the activities of the day. This section is further divided in four other segments (see Fig. 6):

Goal: the objective of the day's theme and activities.
Personal: an individual task assigned to the user.
Group: an activity to conduct in groups, with both adults and pupils.
Reflection: self-assessment questions, analyzing the successfulness of the activities and helping the users reflect on them.

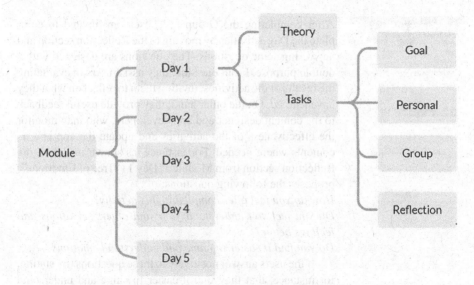

Fig. 6. PSsmile App modules' general structure

As an example, consider the activities in the PSsmile first module **Self-Awareness.** It is divided into the following five daily activities: *Tree of Emotions; My strengths, My Uniqueness; Strengths Chain; Let it Out; Snap Future Me!*

Starting from Day 1 of Module 1: *"Tree of Emotions"*, the users begin their journey towards stronger socio-emotional skills by learning new vocabulary on how to better express and understand their own emotions. The self-directed exercise asks them to look at an image of people climbing a tree and describe their feelings. Supported by Plutchik's "Wheel of Emotions" (see Fig. 7), app users will become able to define nuanced emotions and feelings.

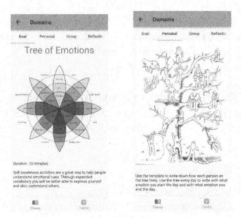

Fig. 7. Day 1 "Tree of Emotions": Goal and Self-Directed exercise

Fig. 8. Day 1 "Tree of Emotions": Reflection section

After completing the Group task, users are invited to complete the Day activities by moving to the Reflection section and answering some questions. The questions are designed with a double purpose. From one side, they assist users in evaluating the results of the activities, inviting them to reflect on what they have learned. On the other hand, they provide useful feedback to the content designer and app developers, who may monitor the effectiveness of the activities and update the app and its contents where needed. For instance, as shown in Fig. 8, the Reflection section from Module 1, Day 1 ("Tree of Emotions") proposes the following questions:

How do you feel after completing this activity?

Do you feel you understand your and others' emotions and feelings better?

Do you find it easier to name and understand emotions?

If the users answer positively to these questions (by stating, for instance, that they find it easier to name and understand emotions), the activities have been successful, the users have improved their socioemotional skills, and the app delivered its purpose.

After answering the questions, users save their progress by clicking on the Save button. The next day, a new day will be available as well as new tasks.

5 PSsmile App in Practice: What to Learn and How to Use It

The app is designed to increase the socio-emotional skills of teachers and parents and, at the same time, help them pass those same skills to their respective pupils and children. +

The strict steps of the app, which requires users to wait one day before proceeding to the subsequent activities, have been implemented with the intention of increasing the skills of the target groups in a gradual but constant way, giving ample space to reflect on the issues addressed in each day. Whether the user is a parent or a teacher, it is highly recommended to stick to the programme, as the activities have been designed to be conducted one after the other, in a consequential manner.

The app is very flexible, as it could be implemented in different contexts, being that at school, at home or even in other educational centers, where children perform additional educational activities and interact with their peers by playing. The group activities for children should always be performed with the supervision of one or more adults, who can steer the dialogue among children and guide them towards a higher understanding of their and other emotions.

Moving from modules to modules, both adult learners and pupils will acquire the following competences:

Self-awareness. Within this module, all learners will increase their *"ability to recognize their own emotions, thoughts, and values and how they influence behavior."* At the end of this module, users will be able to:

- Identify personal, cultural, and linguistic assets.
- Identify personal emotions.
- Link feelings, values, and thoughts.
- Examine prejudices and biases.

Self-management. Through this module, users will learn how to regulate their own emotions, thoughts, and behaviors in different situations. This includes also better stress management, control of impulses, and increased motivation. Specific skills of people with prominent levels of self-awareness include also:

- Positive management of emotions.
- The ability to delay gratification.
- Identification and adoption of stress management strategies.
- Acceptance of difficulties as positive challenges.

Social Awareness. In the third module of the app, learners will increase their ability to understand others' emotions, and improve their empathy, particularly towards those with diverse backgrounds and cultures. Related sub-competencies are:

- Good listening and attention to emotional cues.
- Recognition of others' strengths.
- Reading of key positive relationships and social networks.
- Accurate reading of social situations and external realities.

Social Management. The fourth module focuses on the improvement of relationship skills, improving learners' ability ability to manage relations with others and the capability of establishing and maintaining healthy and supportive relationships with different individuals and groups. Prominent levels of relationship skills are often associated to:

- The ability to analyze situations and cooperatively find solutions.
- Pro-social behaviors.
- Active citizenship.
- High sociability.

Decision Making and Future Goals Setting. This last module addresses the overarching components of the PSsmile framework, which includes elements of awareness and management. For this reason, they are addressed in all the previous modules, thus helping the learners practice the skills learned in everyday situations. Users are expected to:

- Increase the ability to take responsible decisions for self and others.
- Establish a positive mindset about themselves and their future.
- Set goals and define strategies to achieve them.

6   PSsmile App – Alpha Testing and Pilot Use

At the current stage, the alpha version is already available on the Google Play Store (https://play.google.com/store/apps/details?id=lt.vrlab.ps_smile), where all project partners and adults in the pilot study had the opportunity to download it and use it. The alpha test involved 2 to 3 staff members from each of the six project partner organizations, which provided qualitative feedback on: The app's structure; The content; The User Experience (UX) design. Key points characterizing the app emerged.

Concerning the *app's structure*, all the twelve persons involved in the testing provided positive feedback, claiming that it is coherent with the general project's goals and the specific goals of the app. The incremental design of the activities was particularly praised, as many participants claimed that it will help users acquire the expected skills quite easily.

Similar opinions were shared regarding the app's *content*, i.e., the theoretical information and the tasks provided. Members from the project partners' team particularly appreciated the variety of single and group activities offered in each domain, which were claimed to be very "*creative, clear in their intentions and effective in developing the expected skills.*" Moreover, the use of multiple sources for the tasks, such as stories, videos, and images, was found to increase users' engagement and was considered "*especially useful for imparting SEL to children.*"

The self-assessment questions available in the "*Reflection*" segment were found to be helpful in expanding the effectiveness of the tasks offered. "*By inviting users to reflect on the exercises carried out, these questions offer them not only the opportunity to evaluate whether the tasks achieved the expected results or not, but they also make them reflect on the goal of the exercises themselves, motivating users to understand SEL process in greater depth.*"

Additionally, specific choices were crucial for the *User Experience (UX) design*:

- *Auditory and visual elements* indicating the completion of the activities. The completion of an activity can be reported by clicking the "*Done*" button collocated at the bottom of each task's page. Sounds and images appear after pressing the button providing immediate feedback on task completion.

– *Feedback on the task completed.* To motivate users, a screen congratulating them for completing the task was effective.
– Module-related *colors.* Every *"Domains"* menu has a specific color for each domain and the completion of the tasks within each domain is reported with the same color or tick.

7 Conclusions

The significant role that schools, and contexts may play in supporting a whole children's development, will be ensured with all members of the community receiving the support that they require, first from the closer significant adults in their life, which is from teachers and parents.

Recent actions implemented to improve and evaluate the *PSsmile* app, although involving project partners who may have some favourable bias and specific knowledge, nonetheless provide evidence of its usefulness and show that thanks to the methodology and the principles adopted, the innovative tool developed is ready to be effectively and simultaneously used by parents and teachers while their primary school' pupils are taking part in the related school curriculum.

A systemic approach involving all members of the educational community can go further to not only support children currently and during future school disruptions, but also all individuals as educators, parents, and responsible adults that take care of their personal and community members' wellbeing.

References

1. Collaborative for Academic, Social, and Emotional Learning: Effective social and emotional learning program. CASEL Guide (2012)
2. Durlak, J.A.: Handbook of Social and Emotional Learning: Research and Practice. Guilford Publications, USA (2015)
3. Cefai, C., Cavioni, V.: From neurasthenia to eudaimonia: Teachers' well-being and resilience. In: Social and Emotional Education in Primary School, pp. 133–148. Springer, New York (2014). https://doi.org/10.1007/978-1-4614-8752-4_8
4. Fischer, S.N.: Teacher perceptions of the social emotional learning standards (2017)
5. Cefai, C., Cooper, P.: Emotional education: Connecting with students thoughts and emotions (2009)
6. Mascheroni, G., Winther, D.K., Saeed, M., Zaffaroni, L.G., Cino, D., Dreesen, T., Valenza, M.: La didattica a distanza durante l'emergenza COVID-19: l'esperienza italiana (No. inorer1191) (2021)
7. Cefai, C., Bartolo, P.A., Cavioni, V., Downes, P.: Strengthening social and Emotional Education as a Core Curricular Area Across the EU: A Review of the International Evidence. Analytical report. Publications Office of the European Union, Luxembourg (2018)
8. Domitrovich, C.E., Durlak, J.A., Staley, K.C., Weissberg, R.P.: Social-emotional competence: an essential factor for promoting positive adjustment and reducing risk in school children. Child Dev. **88**(2), 408–416 (2017)

9. Pomerance, L., Greenberg, J., Walsh, K.: Learning about Learning: What Every New Teacher Needs to Know. National Council on Teacher Quality, Washington, D.C. (2016)
10. Dusenbury, L., Zadrazil, J., Mart, A., Weissberg, R.: State Learning Standards to Advance Social and Emotional Learning. CASEL, Chicago (2011)
11. Elias, M.J., Leverett, L., Duffell, J.C., Humphrey, N., Stepney, C., Ferrito, J.: Integrating SEL with related prevention and youth development approaches (2015)
12. Weissberg, R.P., O'Brien, M.U.: What works in school-based social and emotional learning programs for positive youth development. Ann. Am. Acad. Pol. Soc. Sci. **591**(1), 86–97 (2004)
13. Zins, J.E., Elias, M.J., Greenberg, M.T.: School practices to build social-emotional competence as the foundation of academic and life success. In: Reuven Bar-On, J.G.M., Maurice J.E. (eds.) Educating People Emotionally Intelligent, pp. 79–94. Praeger Publishers (2007)
14. Jennings, P.A., Doyle, S., Oh, Y., Rasheed, D., Frank, J.L., Brown, J.L.: Long-term impacts of the CARE program on teachers' self-reported social and emotional competence and well-being. J. Sch. Psychol. **76**, 186–202 (2019)
15. Sheridan, S.M., Witte, A.L., Holmes, S.R., Wu, C., Bhatia, S.A., Angell, S.R.: The efficacy of conjoint behavioural consultation in the home setting: outcomes and mechanisms in rural communities. J. Sch. Psychol. **62**, 81–101 (2017)
16. Smith, T.E., Reinke, W.M., Herman, K.C., Huang, F.: Understanding family–school engagement across and within elementary-and middle-school contexts. School Psychology **34**(4), 363 (2019)
17. Sheridan, S.M., Smith, T.E., Moorman Kim, E., Beretvas, S.N., Park, S.: A meta-analysis of family-school interventions and children's social-emotional functioning: moderators and components of efficacy. Rev. Educ. Reș. **89**(2), 296–332 (2019)
18. Organisation for Economic Co-operation and Development: Skills for Social Progress: The Power of Social and Emotional Skills. OECD Publishing (2015)
19. Elliott, S.N., Anthony, C.J., Lei, P.W., DiPerna, J.C.: Parents' assessment of students' social emotional learning competencies: the SSIS SEL brief scales-parent version. Family Relat. **71**, 1102–1121 (2021)
20. Thompson, R., Happold, C.: The roots of school readiness in social and emotional development. Kauffman Early Educ. Exch. **1**, 8–29 (2002)
21. Elliott, S.N., Lei, P.W., Anthony, C.J., DiPerna, J.C.: Screening the whole social-emotional child: expanding a brief SEL assessment to include emotional behavior concerns. School Psychol. Rev. **52**, 1–15 (2020)
22. Sanders, M.R., Mazzucchelli, T.G.: The promotion of self-regulation through parenting interventions. Clin. Child. Fam. Psychol. Rev. **16**(1), 1–17 (2013). https://doi.org/10.1007/s10567-013-0129-z
23. Lerner, R.M., et al.: Positive youth development: processes, programs, and problematics. J. Youth Dev. **6**(3), 38–62 (2011)
24. Oluremi, F.D.: Attitude of teachers to students with special needs in mainstreamed public secondary schools in southwestern Nigeria: the need for a change. Eur. Sci. J. **11**(10), 194–209 (2015)
25. Gillespie, C.: 10 apps to help kids control their emotions, Mashable (2018)
26. Morganti, A., Pascoletti, S., Signorelli, A.: Per un'educazione inclusiva: la sfida innovativa delle tecnologie per l'educazione socio-emotiva. Form@ re, 16(3) (2016)
27. Stern, R.S., Harding, T.B., Holzer, A.A., Elbertson, N.A.: Current and potential uses of technology to enhance SEL: what's now and what's next. Handbook of social and emotional learning: Research and practice, pp. 516–531 (2015)

28. Sgaramella, T.M., Ferrari, L., Drąsutė, V.: social and emotional education: a review of applied research studies and curricula and proposal for an integrative approach. Appl. Psychol. Around World **77**, 77 (2020)

29. Bortoluzzi, M., Sgaramella, T. M., Ferrari, L., Drąsutė, V., Šarauskytė, V.: Building emotionally stable, inclusive, and healthy communities with ICT: from state of the art to PSsmile app. In: Pires, I. M., Spinsante, S., Zdravevski, E., Lameski, P. (eds.) GOODTECHS 2021. LNICSSITE, vol. 401, pp. 163–178. Springer, Cham (2021). https://doi.org/10.1007/978-3-030-91421-9_13

Haptic-Based Cognitive Mapping to Support Shopping Malls Exploration

Maria Teresa Paratore⬥ and Barbara Leporini(✉)⬥

ISTI-CNR Area della Ricerca di Pisa, 56124 Pisa, Italy
{mariateresa.paratore,barbara.leporini}@isti.cnr.it

Abstract. This paper describes a study, which is currently underway, whose aim is to investigate how the haptic channel can be effectively exploited by visually impaired users in a mobile app for the preliminary exploration of an indoor environment, namely a shopping mall. Our goal was to use haptics to convey knowledge of how the points of interest (POIs) are distributed within the physical space, and at the same time provide information about the function of each POI, so that users can get a perception of how functional areas are distributed in the environment "at a glance". Shopping malls are typical indoor environments in which orientation aids are highly appreciated by customers, and many different functional areas persist. We identified seven typical categories of POIs which can be encountered in a mall, and then associated a different vibration pattern each. In order to validate our approach, we designed and developed a prototype for preliminary testing, based on the Android platform. The prototype was periodically debugged with the aid of two visually impaired experienced users, who gave us precious advice throughout the development process. We will describe how this app was conceived, the issues emerged during its development and the positive outcomes produced by a very early testing stage. Finally, we will show that the proposed approach is promising and is worthy of further investigation.

Keywords: Haptic feedback · User interfaces · Accessibility · Mobile applications · Orientation and mobility · Indoor exploration · Cognitive maps

1 Introduction

Mobile applications for navigation have been growing more and more popular over the latest years and are now considered essential utilities on every smartphone. Positioning services such as those provided by Google Maps [1] or OpenStreetMap [2] are widely adopted by developers in order to build applications dealing with the Internet of Things (IoT) and Smart Cities environments. Navigation apps have proven to be effective assistive solutions for persons with visual impairments, helping them achieve better social inclusion and autonomy [3]. While visiting an indoor or outdoor environment, visually impaired users can rely upon a navigation app to get real-time information about their actual position, route planning, and accessibility warnings, so that they can get to a specific place in the safest and more effective way. An overview of indoor navigation aids for persons with visual impairments is provided in [13].

I. M. Pires et al. (Eds.): GOODTECHS 2022, LNICST 476, pp. 54–62, 2023.
https://doi.org/10.1007/978-3-031-28813-5_4

In this paper, we are investigating digital maps meant to provide visually impaired users with a "mental overview" of the environment before physically accessing it. A typical use case might be planning a visit to a mall to make a series of purchases. A shopping mall is a very complex building in which it is important to distinguish specific functional areas, such as ATMs, information centers, bars and obviously the different types of shops. Any mall nowadays provides visitors with digital maps, through its website or a dedicated mobile app, however, as far as we know, these aids are not accessible for visually impaired users.

A cognitive, or mental, map is a mental representation of the spatial environment that the human brain builds as a memory aid, in order to support future actions. A cognitive map is leveraged by the human brain during spatial navigation. A neurological insight of this process is provided by Epstein et al. in [4], in which authors highlight that cognitive mapping accounts for three basic elements, spatial coding, landmark anchoring and route planning. An effective cognitive map allows a subject to localize and orient themselves in the space in relation to the landmarks and elaborate a route to reach a given point in the environment. Building a cognitive map, thus, implies developing skills to understand the structure and function of an environment, and to describe its organization and relations with other physical spaces [3]; it is a process of gaining awareness of a physical environment, so it is useful in a training phase before accessing an unfamiliar place. An app that helps to form a mental map, therefore, should not be understood as a tool that guides the user step-by-step in real time, but rather as a tool to be used in advance to facilitate a visit and plan an itinerary through a complex environment.

Hardcopy tactile maps are commonly used to support the development of cognitive maps for visually impaired users [5, 6]. The haptic channel, anyway, has been proven to be as effective as the tactile feedback [7], especially when adopted together with the audio channel [5].

Traditionally, haptics has been used to provide information about dangerous spots, obstacles, crossroads and other physical barriers [3]. Studies on wearable systems exist, which involve the use of the haptic channel to convey instructions on movement. Bharadwaj et al. [8] investigated the usage of a hip-worn vibrating belt to convey turn signals while walking through an unknown route, and their findings suggest the effectiveness of haptics as a notification channel in noisy environments when using a navigation aid.

Papadopoulos et al. [5], investigated how different modalities of exploring a map affect the spatial knowledge acquired by the users. In particular, three modalities of exploration were considered; a verbal description of the physical environment, an audio-tactile map rendered via a touchpad, and an audio-haptic map where the haptic feedback was provided through a commercial, portable haptic device. During the exploration, different feedbacks were associated to streets, POIs and dangerous locations, in order to help distinguish among them. Moreover, a soundscape was associated to intersections. Results of the study highlight how tactile and haptic feedbacks, associated with the audio channel, can improve the mental representation of physical space, compared to systems in which only audio feedbacks are adopted.

As tablets and smartphones have become increasingly powerful and versatile, several studies have explored the possibility of using digital counterparts of tactile maps, obtained by exploiting mobile devices' haptic, audio and text-to-speech capabilities and taking advantage of the assistive technologies provided by the mobile devices' operating systems.

Palani et al. [9] developed an experimental digital map for the formation of a cognitive spatial representation based on the haptic and audio channels. Authors performed a series of tests with sighted and visually impaired users, aimed at assessing the validity of the digital map with respect to traditional mapping methods (visual and hardcopy-vibration). Their study shows that a digital vibro-audio map provides equivalent performances than traditional mapping methods for both categories of users. Analogous results were achieved in [10], where authors investigate the learning and wayfinding performances obtained by visually impaired users equipped with digital maps for the preliminary exploration of unknown indoor environments. In both studies, vibrations are used to help users acquire knowledge of the physical space, but scarce or no attention is paid to provide information about POIs.

The use of vibration patterns to convey information through the haptic channel was explored in [11] to delimit logical partitions of the screen with different functions, while in [12] Gonzalez-Canete et al. Showed that different vibration patterns associated to haptic icons improve the process of learning the icons' locations on a touchscreen and the icon recognition rate for both sighted and visually impaired users.

Our study aims at investigating the potentialities of vibration patterns to convey information about the position and function of a POI, thus enhancing the learning rate of a cognitive map. The novelty of our approach is to adopt the haptic channel in order to provide not only spatial cognition, but also an overview of the functional areas of the environment. This paper describes the preliminary phase of our study, in which a mobile Android application for testing purposes was designed and developed with the aid of two visually impaired users. Our reference use case was "planning a visit to an unknown mall", however our approach can be generalized to any indoor environments or even outdoors.

2   The Test Application

Our test application provides users with a simple audio-vibration map of a shopping mall. Seven functional categories of POIs were identified, which are typical of the target environment, and each category was associated with a different vibration pattern.

The map was developed by overlapping two layers, i.e. two PNG images, one of which is invisible (hidden) to the end user. The invisible layer is responsible for the haptic and audio rendering, while the other one is used for visualization purposes; in fact, it is a black and white representation of the environment containing the POIs and their descriptive labels (i.e. short descriptions). The hidden layer is formed by a set of colored areas, each corresponding to a POI, as shown in Fig. 1.

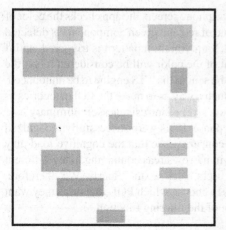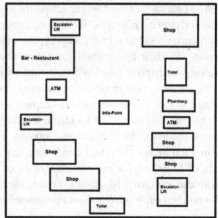

Fig. 1. The map used for our tests and the corresponding representation, internal to the app, in which functional areas are characterized by different colors.

We adopted RGB color encoding to identify POIs and provide information about their categories. A color scheme for our application was in fact defined in such a way that each POI category corresponded to a fixed couple of Red and Green levels. The Blue component, on the other hand, was used to precisely identify each single POI and was associated with a descriptive label, e.g. the name of a shop. According to this strategy, hence, each category can account for up to 256 different POIs.

Figure 2 depicts a code snippet of the application, in which POI categories and the related vibration patterns are declared. Vibration patterns are encoded, as required by Android, as arrays of long integers, that are taken as arguments by the functions of the operating system's vibration service. Vibration patterns associated to the different categories are described in an intuitive form in Table 1, in which the dash identifies a 100 ms pause, and the terms "short", "long" and "longer" identify 100, 200, and 300 ms vibrations respectively.

Table 1. Vibration patterns associated to POI categories and the correspondent descriptions sent to the TTS service.

Category	Pattern	Verbal description
ATM	short vib.-longer vib	"ATM"
TOILET	longer vib. –long vib	"Toilet facilities"
INFODESK	longer vib. –long vib. –longer vib	"Information desk"
SHOP	short vib	"Shop"
STAIRS_ELEVATOR	short vib.-short vib.-short vib	"Stairs or elevator"
PHARMACY	long vib. –short vib. –short vib	"Pharmacy"
BAR_RESTAURANT	longer vib	"Bar or restaurant"

As a user swipes their finger across the smartphone screen, the app checks the color of the underlying coordinates. Whenever a couple of red and green components is detected which correspond to a POI category, the matching vibration pattern is triggered, and if the user lifts their finger, the Blue component of the color will be considered to get the matching descriptive label, which in turn will be sent to the TTS engine to be announced.

We strove to design vibration patterns in such a way as to make the POI categories as distinguishable as possible while keeping a low level of intrusiveness. Preliminary user tests highlighted that, after an initial training phase, POIs were successfully recognized through the associated vibrations, anyway a concern arose that the cognitive load may become too heavy in certain conditions (e.g. in narrow areas containing many different kinds of POIs) or for certain categories of users, such as the elderly. We, therefore, introduced a filtering function to enable users to choose which POI categories they want to be notified of. Figure 3 shows a screenshot of the filtering function.

```
<!-- color correspondences -->
<color name="pharmacy">#FFFF88</color>
<color name="info_box">#80D8A8</color>
<color name="stairs_elevator">#89DAE5</color>
<color name="shop">#ABCCF6</color>
<color name="atm">#BCC8CE</color>
<color name="bar_restaurant">#FFC90E</color>
<color name="toilettes">#F7B8C8</color>
```

```
//pattern values in nsecs
public static long[] PATTERN PHARMACY = new Long[] {8, LONG_VIB, PAUSE, SHORT_VIB, PAUSE, SHORT_VIB};
public static long[] PATTERN INFOBOX = new long[]{0, LONGER_VIB, PAUSE, LONG_VIB, PAUSE, LONGER VIB);
public static long[] PATTERN STAIRSELEVATOR = new long[] {e, SHORT_VIB, PAUSE, SHORT_VIB, PAUSE, SHORT_VIB};
public static long[] PATTERN SHOP= new long[] {0, SHORT_VIB};
public static long[] PATTERN TOILETTE= new long[]{0, LONGER_VIB, PAUSE, LONG_VIB};
public static long[] PATTERN_ATH = new long[]{0, SHORT_VIB, PAUSE, LONGER_VIB};
public static long[] PATTERN RESTAURANT = new long[]{0, LONGER_VIB};
```

Fig. 2. Code snippets that show how colors correspondences and vibration patterns are defined programmatically.

Users were asked to evaluate three alternative modalities of feedback; audio only, vibration only, audio and vibration. Table 2 compares the different behavior of the app when a POI is hovered in the three different modalities of interaction. In any case, lifting the finger in correspondence of a POI triggers the announcement of the POI's short description.

Fig. 3. The function to filter through the POI categories.

Table 2. The three interaction modes of the app and the corresponding haptic behavior when a POI area is hovered.

Mode	Behavior
VIBRATION	A vibration pattern hint is issued
AUDIO	A vocal hint is issued announcing the category type
AUDIO AND VIBRATION	A vocal hint is issued together with a vibration pattern

Figure 4 shows a screenshot of the app with the three buttons to switch between the different modalities on the upper right corner, and the button to filter through POI categories on the bottom. In order to enable visually impaired users to easily switch between the modalities of interaction without the aid of a screen reader, we associated a "toggle mode" function to the double-tap gesture. For this preliminary version of the app, we did not consider the use of Android's default screen reader (TalkBack), since it posed development issues, due to known bugs, that went beyond the scope of our study.

Due to the COVID-19 pandemic situation, we were not able to carry out extensive structured tests at the time of writing. Sessions for preliminary evaluation and debugging were held remotely via Skype instead of in person, as we had planned. Two experienced visually impaired users (i.e. users accustomed to using the smartphone as a daily aid to their independence) installed the app on their devices; unfortunately, remote testing did not make it possible to involve users that were less skilled in using the smartphone. Users were asked to explore the same map of the ground floor of a shopping mall, unknown to both of them, by interacting with the app in each of the three modalities.

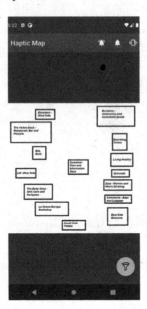

Fig. 4. A screenshot of the app used for testing.

2.1 Preliminary Evaluation

The app was developed on a HUAWEI T5 Mediapad tablet with a 10.1″ display, running Android 8.0. Accessibility and usability debugging sessions were held remotely on a TCL 20S, and a Google Pixel 3, both running Android 11, with a 6.67″ and a 6,3″ display, respectively.

Overall, we found that, by exploring the map through the application, users were able to get an idea of the arrangement of the POIs and had no difficulty in recalling the location of specific POIs, as well as the total number of shops, entrances and stairs. The task of finding a given shop on the map was also successfully accomplished. The map was correctly rendered on their devices and the vibration patterns were correctly perceived, while problems were occasionally noticed with the TTS hints. Our users pointed out that the audio hints were often missing and they had to repeat the exploration of the area surrounding the POI, two or three times before having an audio response. This behavior was probably due to differences in the TTS engines, but we could not reproduce it, so it needs further investigations.

The "audio and vibration" mode was considered "overwhelming". Users declared they would rather not use it as a "standard" modality of interaction, but only in a preliminary phase, when correspondences between vibration patterns and POI categories must be learnt. Speaking of audio feedback, users declared that it may be worth trying to have less intrusive, non-verbal "audio icons" associated to POI categories. Users also suggested that the stereo audio channels could be exploited to reproduce this kind of icons, in such a way to indicate the direction of the related POIs. The feature of filtering among POI categories was also highly appreciated, anyway it was highlighted that POIs related to obstacles or potentially dangerous structural elements (such as stairs) should always be shown on the map, and users should not be enabled to filter them out.

Finally, a "zoom and pagination" feature was required for a later version of the app, since vibration hints related to close POIs in narrow areas occasionally generated confusion and required repeated explorations. For the map under test, this phenomenon had a fairly limited impact, but for more complex maps, e.g. relating to urban environments, a zooming function that could also divide the space into separately navigable areas was suggested as very helpful.

3 Open Issues and Future Work

Besides the bugs signaled by our users, which are strictly platform-dependent, the major open issues we will face before releasing the app for testing to a wide audience are those related to the "zooming and pagination feature". Integration with TalkBack, albeit not fundamental for evaluating the validity of our approach, will also be implemented, in order to allow an easier execution of the tests to a greater number of users.

Regarding the use of the haptic channel, further ad hoc trials will be carried out, focusing on specific aspects such as the maximum number of patterns that can be used at the same time and the most effective pause and vibration configurations. In particular, we will analyze correlations between the users' demographic data and their preferred patterns. The need to hold the tests remotely prevented us from involving users who were less experienced in the use of digital technologies. In the upcoming tests, we will involve also this crucial category of users. Finally, the extension of the presented approach to outdoor maps provided by services such as OpenStreetMap is already the subject of an ongoing study.

4 Conclusions

We have presented a novel approach to exploit the haptic channel in order to help users with visual impairments build mental representations of a physical space. In particular, we focused our attention on mobile applications as a means of building cognitive maps. A mobile application to explore a shopping mall was developed for testing purposes and evaluated by two visually impaired users. Vibration patterns were used to indicate positions and functions of distinct areas in the shopping mall, together with more traditional audio cues; comparisons between different modalities of interaction were carried out. Overall, our approach has proven sound and promising for the future. Of course, more extensive testing needs to be done, involving many more users and more effective functionalities. To this end, we have highlighted the problems that are still open and how we intend to solve them. Finally, we have described possible ways to exploit the potentialities of our study in the near future.

Acknowledgments. This work was funded by the Italian Ministry of Research through the research projects of national interest (PRIN) TIGHT (Tactile InteGration for Humans and arTificial systems).

References

1. Google Maps website: https://developers.google.com/maps?hl=en
2. OpenStreetMap website: https://www.openstreetmap.org/about
3. Khan, A., Khusro, S.: An insight into smartphone-based assistive solutions for visually impaired and blind people: issues, challenges and opportunities. Univ. Access Inf. Soc. **20**(2), 265–298 (2020). https://doi.org/10.1007/s10209-020-00733-8
4. Epstein, R.A., Patai, E.Z., Julian, J.B., Spiers, H.J.: The cognitive map in humans: spatial navigation and beyond. Nat. Neurosci. **20**, 1504–1513 (2017)
5. Papadopoulos, K., Koustriava, E., Koukourikos, P., et al.: Comparison of three orientation and mobility aids for individuals with blindness: Verbal description, audio-tactile map and audio-haptic map. Assist. Technol. **29**, 1–7 (2017)
6. Espinosa, M.A., Ochaita, E.: Using tactile maps to improve the practical spatial knowledge of adults who are blind. J. Vis. Impairment Blindness **92**, 338–345 (1998)
7. Saket, B., Prasojo, C., Huang, Y., Zhao, S.: Designing an effective vibration-based notification interface for mobile phones. In: Proceedings of the 2013 Conference on Computer Supported Cooperative Work (2013)
8. Bharadwaj, A., Shaw, S., Goldreich, D.:Comparing tactile to auditory guidance for blind individuals. Front. Hum. Neurosci. **13** (2019)
9. Palani, H.P., Fink, P.D., Giudice, N.A.: Comparing map learning between touchscreen-based visual and haptic displays: a behavioral evaluation with blind and sighted users. Multimodal Technol. Interact. **6**(1) (2021)
10. Giudice, N.A., Guenther, B.A., Jensen, N.A., and Haase, K.N.: Cognitive mapping without vision: comparing wayfinding performance after learning from digital touchscreen-based multimodal maps vs. embossed tactile overlays. Front. Hum. Neurosci. **14** (2020)
11. Buzzi, M., Buzzi, M., Leporini, B., Paratore, M.T.: Vibro-tactile enrichment improves blind user interaction with mobile touchscreens. In Proceedings of the 14th IFIP Conference on Human-Computer Interaction, Cape Town, South Africa, 2–6 September 2013
12. González-Cañete, F.J., López-Rodríguez, J.L., Galdón, P.M., Estrella, A.D.: Improving the screen exploration of smartphones using haptic icons for visually impaired users. Sensors **21** (2021)
13. Ryu, H., Kim, T., Li, K.: Indoor navigation map for visually impaired people. ISA 2014 (2014)

Towards Design Recommendations for Social Engagement Platforms Supporting Volunteerism Targeting Older People in Local Communities

Renny S. N. Lindberg$^{(\boxtimes)}$ (iD), Beat Signer (iD), and Olga De Troyer (iD)

Web and Information Systems Engineering Lab, Vrije Universiteit Brussel,
Pleinlaan 2, 1050 Brussels, Belgium
{rlindber,bsigner,odetroye}@vub.be

Abstract. COVID-19 showed the need for community support networks to help vulnerable individuals that were forced to stay in their homes during extended periods. While the pandemic is slowly passing, there is still a need for this type of help, especially for elderly who nowadays want to live longer in their own home. Several social engagement platforms are already offering support for this type of services. However, some became rather inactive, while others are successful but not always in the context of offering help to vulnerable elderly. In this paper we present 16 design recommendations to consider when designing (or to improve) social engagement platforms focused on volunteerism for helping older people. These recommendations are based on the evaluation of 10 digital social engagement platforms that allow asking for assistance and/or volunteering to provide help.

Keywords: Social engagement · Volunteerism digital platforms · Design recommendations

1 Introduction

The COVID-19 pandemic that is now active for over two years (since emerging in early 2020) has revealed and worsened several societal issues. The quarantines and measures implemented by governments in order to combat the disease have been discussed in media and literature ever since, focusing in particular on adverse effects of isolation [2,12,13,15]. These measures and "lockdowns" placed a number of vulnerable people—especially the elderly population—in a precarious situation. Being particularly vulnerable, the elderly were largely forced to stay at home and ordinary shopping trips turned into an ordeal. However, this situation did not go unnoticed and several existing digital social engagement (SE) platforms and local outreach programs attempted to provide assistance to this problem. SE platforms are intended to digitally support social

I. M. Pires et al. (Eds.): GOODTECHS 2022, LNICST 476, pp. 63–79, 2023.
https://doi.org/10.1007/978-3-031-28813-5_5

engagement. Social engagement itself can be seen as a broad definition for members of a community interacting with each other. Our definition for social engagement (SE) is *"social engagement is the commitment of a member to stay in the group and interact with other members"* and is based on a definition provided by Zhang et al. [17]. On an SE platform, the interaction between people is enabled digitally. SE platforms are in the right position to offer support for people willing to help each other.

Several SE platforms existed already for a while, including Nappi Naapuri (Finland), Nextdoor (USA), Nebenan (Germany), and Hoplr (Belgium). Additionally, Facebook recently launched their own Help Hub, and similar services, such as Commu (Finland) and Nachbarschaft (Germany), were established during the COVID-19 pandemic.

While most SE platforms are initially successful, after a while they disappear or become far less active. In addition, for the ones that have a good number of users, the type of help provided seems to be more focused on giving advise rather than on physically helping each other. The aim of our work was to investigate why this is the case and how we could improve the engagement and retention of users, especially in the context of helping each other with daily tasks. For this purpose, we investigated several SE platforms. Based on the findings, we formulate a number of design recommendations to improve user engagement and retention of SE platforms targeting volunteerism to help elderly people. The focus of the paper is on these recommendations.

The remainder of the paper is structured as follows. We start in Sect. 2 by presenting the methodology for deriving the recommendations, which is based on the evaluation of existing SE platforms. In Sect. 3 we present the different SE platforms selected for evaluation and provide some information about the evaluations. In Sect. 4 we introduce the design recommendations derived from our findings, and end by providing conclusions.

2   Methodology

We first describe how the existing SE platforms to be evaluated were identified and then present the different methods used to analyse them.

2.1   Finding and Selecting Social Engagement Platforms

Our focus in searching for SE platforms was on active platforms, meaning that platforms that were no longer active were ignored. The main method of discovering platforms was by a query on Google using the keywords: "neighborhood", "community", "social engagement", "neighbor" and "local". These were amended with additional help words, such as "app", "application", "technology" or "platform". The discovered SE platforms were checked for their suitability using the following two criteria: whether (1) a user is able to ask for help and/or to respond to such a help request using the platform, and (2) whether this service is available for free.

2.2   Evaluations Methods

The SE platforms were evaluated by means of a hands-on evaluation, interviews, and user surveys. The purpose of the hands-on evaluation was to inspect which features a platform offers and how. For this, we used an existing design guideline list [10]. Interviews were conducted with platform representatives. The role of the interviews was to get an overview of the aims and goals of the platforms, potential design hurdles, and their opinions on the users and the field of digital volunteering. The interviews were carried out in a semi-structured manner where we started with a number of fixed questions but conversations were allowed to diverge from the original questions. User surveys were conducted on three SE platforms with the aim of seeing how actively users actually helped one another and getting other relevant user trends and opinions about the platforms' features.

After the initial check for suitability, requests for interviews were sent out to the platforms deemed suitable. We performed interviews with representatives of five SE platforms: Commu, Hoplr, ¿Tienes Sal?, Nappi Naapuri, and Solidare-it!. User surveys were conducted on three of these SE platforms, including Commu, Nappi Naapuri, and Hoplr. Note that the surveys were not identical, but adapted to the context of the platforms. However, all surveys were roughly of the same length and took around 20 min to fill in. The tool used for handling the surveys was Qualtrics[1]. The complete survey and interview transcripts (questions and results) can be found online[2].

Some platforms also offer a mobile app for their service, and in the case of Commu, this is the only version they offer. In terms of our evaluation, findings about the applications are considered as a whole, unless specified otherwise. Note that we have anonymized the platforms when discussing individual findings derived either by means of an interview or by a user survey. This was done on the request of some of the platform representatives. When discussing a platform in this manner we use the following acronyms P1, P2, P3, P4, and P5[3]. However, findings that can be concluded from inspecting the platform are not anonymized.

Note that in this paper we do not discuss the different evaluations in great detail as the focus is on the recommendations. The findings which have contributed to the formulation of a recommendation are provided in a motivation preceding each recommendation. Details about the evaluations themselves can be found in [9]. Further, some figures about the participants in the user surveys are given in the next section.

3   Evaluated Social Engagement Platforms

A total of 10 SE platforms were discovered as illustrated in Table 1. A short description of each platform is given below. Note that we could not perform

---

[1] https://www.qualtrics.com.

[2] https://doi.org/10.6084/m9.figshare.19165283.

[3] There is no correspondence with the platform sequence earlier in the text.

a full evaluation of all discovered platforms, as some were country locked and require a local address or phone number. Table 1 also mentions the types of investigation conducted for the individual platforms: Hands-on evaluation (H), interviewing a representative from the platform (I), and performing a survey with platform users (S).

Table 1. SE platforms discovered for our evaluation

Name	Type of platform	(H)ands-on (I)nterview (S)urvey
Allo Voisin	Web, mobile	H (partial evaluation)
Commu	Mobile	H, I, S
Facebook Community Help	Web, mobile	H
Help Your Neighbor	Web	H
Nappi Naapuri	Web	H, I, S
Nachbarschaft	Web	H
Nextdoor	Web, mobile	H (partial evaluation)
¿Tienes Sal?	Web, mobile	H, I
Hoplr	Web, mobile	H, I, S
Solidare-it!	Web	H, I

Allo Voisin[4] is a French platform for provision of services and rental of equipment between neighbors. To register, users need to have a French phone number and address. Therefore, we were unable to create an account on the platform, but the platform allows viewing the main forum. It is unclear how large the number of Allo Voisin users is that use the platform for simply helping each other, as it is more driven towards small businesses and earning money on the side. However, as it can also be used for helping each other, we have included it in our list. In terms of functionality, the platform offers relatively simple messaging functionality of posting requests for specific tasks.

Commu[5] is a Finnish startup, launched in May 2021. They are currently focusing on two cities in Finland—Tampere and Helsinki— but are aiming to expand. Unlike the other considered platforms, Commu only provides a mobile application. Commu does not have "closed neighborhood forums", but allows making help and requests and offers on the go. Commu allowed users to ask for a small compensation for helping, intended for covering any costs, such as transportation costs. However, this feature has been removed.

Facebook[6] with nearly two billion active users in 2021 needs little introduction. It is a web platform that has shaped how a group of people see and interact with each other, both in good and bad ways. A less well-known feature

---

[4] https://www.allovoisins.com.
[5] https://commuapp.fi.
[6] https://www.facebook.com.

is Facebook's "community help" that was quietly launched during the pandemic outbreak in 2020. It is unclear how Facebook intends to extend this service, but currently it provides simple help and offers request functionalities as a slightly modified version of the regular posting functionality.

Help Your Neighbor[7] is an US-based website focusing on neighborhood-level community building and help finding services. It divides its communication platform into four tiers: individuals, groups, neighborhood, and city. The platform appears to have either very limited activity or has already become inactive. The level of activity remained unclear as Help Your Neighbor is up and running but we did not manage to find very active communities. The platform does require a US zip code as part of the registration process, but this is not checked in any way, as we easily managed to create an account on the platform.

Nachbarshaft[8] is a German website launched during the COVID-19 outbreak as a service to offer help to people affected by the quarantine procedures. It is unclear how active the platform is, but it appears to have some level of activity and being under constant development. The service is limited to Germany.

Nappi Naapuri[9] is a Finnish web platform that, like Commu, provides open access to users. The user must only provide an address, which dictates the general point of focus when logging in. Users may also give multiple addresses. The platform is still up and running, but currently not under active development apart from basic maintenance.

Nextdoor[10] is a US-based service that has also entered the European market[11]. The platform is currently active in 11 countries and is by far the most successful neighborhood application we have looked at.

¿Tienes Sal?[12] is a branch of a German-based company called *Nebenan* that is located in Spain. Nebenan has another branch in France under the name *Mesvoisins*. The service appears to be quite similar to that of Nextdoor with a relatively rigorous registration process where the location of a user is verified by letter, image of a document, or GPS location.

Hoplr[13] is a Belgian-based platform that is rather similar to Nextdoor and Nebenan, also in how they verify their users' domiciles upon registration. They currently advertise 500 000 registered users and are active in Belgium and the Netherlands.

Solidare-it![14] is a Belgian platform, currently mainly utilized by a volunteer organization located in Brussels as an internal database to keep track of their volunteers and people needing help. The platform was originally devised and is still partly marketed as a platform for looking for and offering help. Note that

---

[7] http://www.helpyourneighbor.com.
[8] https://nachbarschaft.care.
[9] https://www.nappinaapuri.fi.
[10] https://nextdoor.nl.
[11] https://techcrunch.com/2017/02/05/streetlife-knocks-nextdoor/.
[12] https://tienes-sal.es.
[13] https://www.hoplr.com.
[14] https://solidare-it.org.

the person interviewed was actually from the volunteer group being the main utilizer of the platform at this time.

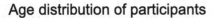

Age distribution of participants

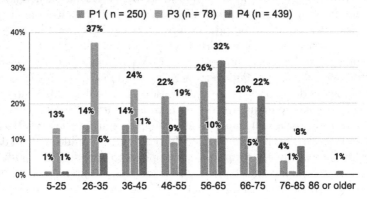

Fig. 1. Age distribution of user survey participants

The age distribution of the responses to our user surveys is shown in Fig. 1. However, it should be mentioned that the number of participants that completed the whole survey was substantially lower: P1 = 149, P3 = 56, P4 = 319.

Table 2. Results for platforms P1, P3 and P4 on whether users asked for or offered help, as well as some feature-specific questions for P4. Neighborhood care is a service where users can openly indicate their willingness to help other users with specific tasks

Platform	n	Question	Neither	Asked help	Offered help	Both
P1	247	*Have you requested/offered help on X?*	62%	10%	21%	7%
P3	59		63%	7%	12%	12%
			No	Yes		
P4	395	*Have you filled in the "How can you help your neighbors?" part in your profile?*	70%	30%	Yes, I have used it	
P4	371	*Were you aware of the "Neighborhood care" feature?*	47%	47%	6%	
			No	Yes	I have asked assistance, but not by using "help requests"	
P4	370	*Have you posted a "Help request" message on P4?*	78%	12%	10%	

Another relevant survey result we want to highlight is the number of participants that declared to have used their platform's "Asking or Providing Help" functionality. The results are shown in Table 2 and indicate the relatively low level of actual usage of the provided help functionality.

4 Recommendations

In the following, we introduce and motivate our design recommendations.

R1: Points With Purpose

Gamification features, such as points, are known to have the potential for achieving a higher level of engagement. Points were utilized in a number of evaluated platforms, but based on our interviews, it often appears as a bit of an afterthought. Most commonly, points are given for posting requests or messages.

In terms of giving value to points (i.e., allow to do something with the points), P4 and P5 do attempt this, as P4 specifically states: "The score indicates a user's 'neighborliness' and willingness to help", but at least, currently, there is no scale attached to their scores, e.g., is "70" a high score?, nor a way of knowing how valuable individual actions are, in terms of points. P5 simply allows users to see a user's previous activity.

However, on these types of platforms, where collective good is a key aspect, gamification might sometimes result in negative reactions. For example, leaderboards can in principle be effective but should be utilized with care. Some users in the surveys for instance mentioned that this would go against the altruistic spirit of the platform. Though gamification might not be intended directly for elderly users, there is some evidence that it can in fact also elicit positive outcomes in them [11], such as improved well-being, positive engagement, social interaction or improved condition. However, care is also needed in not making the gamification too difficult to learn for these people.

Recommendation: Our recommendation is to attach (more) clearly defined value to points. Combining points with clear rewards, rather than obscure levels of activity, can be efficient and is a rather common approach on commercial platforms and therefore well known by many users. Some users might not care about collecting points, but even if only a quarter of the users see this as added value, it can become a powerful new avenue for more engaged users.

R2: Show Activity

An active community can stimulate users to be active as well. In the context of helping each other, it could be useful to show how active the platform is in this respect. Currently, none of the platforms communicate about the status of help requests to users, nor utilize any clear methods of internal tracking of the status of help requests, i.e., whether they have been completed or are still active.

Users of P4 have a general level of understanding on how many of their local neighbors are on the platform, but this does not indicate how active they are. Most platforms show activities on an individual message level, but currently it is not easy for users to grasp the overall activity of their neighborhood. In the case of platforms where a geographical map is an integral part of the user interface, this is slightly different as the notifications are clearly visible on the map. But even this comes with its own challenges. An area with few users but a relatively high level of activity might appear quieter than in reality, and in areas with more notifications it might be difficult to ascertain how active the user base is in weekly or monthly terms. Also, such a map can easily clutter the user interface and be less usable on small screens.

Recommendation: Our recommendation is to provide an easy to understand overview of the activity in a user's neighborhood. Depending on how this is done, it can also be utilized in a more meaningful manner. Simple statistics showing past actions by users can be enough, but if this is done graphically and in a playful way, such as by means of a simplified animated graphical representation of the nearby area that changes over time based on user activity, such an animation could be a reason for users to check in regularly, even when they might not have any direct request at that moment. This in turn would help the user to stay connected with the platform. Hoplr seems to be an interesting case in this respect, by showing its users the overall percentage of users who joined from the neighborhood and by providing numerous suggestions on how the user can try to get more people involved.

R3: Guiding Users

Appropriate guiding of users in how to perform tasks is essential for their independence, especially for elderly. The evaluated platforms attempt to instruct their users in how to succeed in tasks in different manners. For simple and more streamlined tasks, this is rather easy as they can simply label the required fields the user needs to fill in, or select the correct radio button. For less straightforward features, this might however not be sufficient. Hence, Hoplr does offer explanations for the different message types, and ¿Tienes Sal? explains the meaning of a "public post". However, these instructive snippets were somewhat intermittent when comparing the platforms approaches. Hoplr, for instance provides suggestions for message content, whereas ¿Tienes Sal? does not. Both offer more detailed instructions on their respective help pages. It is likely safe to assume that the amount of information provided by both platforms is enough for most users. However, cases can be made for needing more detailed guidance. For instance, in the case of ¿Tienes Sal? when making a help request, it is not instantaneously clear which message type the user needs to select, as the help request type is under the "seek" message type, after which the "help & service" needs to be selected.

Recommendation: An unobtrusive guidance that clearly indicates fields that need to be filled in is already mostly used by all the platforms. Our recommendation is to cover all aspects of a task, such as also uploading an image or file, and to provide a direct access to more information. Currently, this information can be found on the help page but such a help page usually needs to be accessed explicitly. Instead, providing a snippet of the help page where it is relevant, might be much more effective and less likely to cause the user to get lost.

R4: Onboarding

Onboarding is a well-known term within the human resources sector where it essentially means "bringing new staff up to speed". Within the domain of UI design for digital technology, onboarding can be seen as a combination of guiding and other design elements, brought together in order to teach the user quickly how to use the application [5]. There are some indications on the importance of well-done onboarding to ensure that users stick with a platform [4] and on improving engagement [14]. The generational gap is also to be considered as more technically savvy users might be divided on the necessity for onboarding [8], but it can be effective in alleviating concerns that elderly users might have [16].

Out of the evaluated platforms, only Commu and Help Your Neighbor appear to provide a more hands-on onboarding session. Commu allows the user to create a dummy help request at the end of the account creation process in order to make the user familiar with this task. Help Your Neighbor highlights and explains all the buttons and most of the icons of each view when first accessing it, but we did not find a way to launch this again at a later stage. A grain of salt is to be added at this point as access to Nextdoor were done via third parties. However, no clear way of activating any onboard-like feature was discovered.

Recommendation: Our recommendation is to offer users a step-by-step onboarding approach. Such an approach has the potential of being a much more effective form of teaching and supporting a novice or elderly user over a large help page. As such an approach may irritate advanced users, the ability to turn it on/off with relative ease is highly recommended. Lastly, there should be an easy way to start the onboarding at will, as sometimes, web services run the onboarding segment only once when first accessing a site, but then hide it.

R5: Usability Guidelines

The importance of following usability guidelines when developing a user interface is well known. No major usability guideline violations were detected when evaluating the platforms, but some minor points of improvement were occasionally detected, such as a lack of confirmation or a summary before posting messages. When interviewing the representatives, for most parts no guidelines were used to ensure usability for elderly users, but despite this, no major issues were detected.

Recommendation: Applying existing usability guidelines when designing an SE platform can provide an important additional mean for ensuring that all usability aspects are covered.

R6: Handling User Feedback

Based on the interviews, feedback handling does appear to be generally functioning well on most of the evaluated platforms. For most parts, this appears to be done via direct emails and by phone. Some level of communication in terms of enhancing the service or informing about well-known bugs is done by emailing users. However, to our knowledge, none of the platforms has a built-in news page that covers bug fixes, or informs on what is currently being worked on. However, maintaining a page on upcoming updates and ensuring the content is clearly written requires quite some resources. Additionally, providing users individual feedback can become difficult when the user base grows. For instance, Commu's insider group can become difficult to control and monitor once the platform grows substantially. Further, it is important to ensure that feedback is not only received from a handful of more engaged members.

Recommendation: It is evident that users want to contact the platform for some of their issues. This is definitely a positive thing, since it may improve the platform. Our recommendation is to (1) provide easy means of giving feedback, (2) keeping track of it, and (3) showing this to users. One such example can be seen from the very successful Star Citizens project that has an open access roadmap[15]. This can also easily become resource heavy from the perspective of the platform, but in the beginning, step (3) can simply be acknowledging the receipt of the feedback. Showcasing that the platform is open for feedback and is actively working on it can not only help to improve usability, but also increase users' trust in the platform.

R7: Audio and Video Messages

Typing a message can become difficult for elderly. Typing text, in particular on smartphone devices, is tedious and error prone even for younger users. For elderly users, larger devices, such as tablets, laptops and desktop computers might mitigate this issue, but elderly can also develop writing problems. An alternative could be to allow them to record a message (audio or video). None of the evaluated platforms offers this functionality. The same applies to reading aloud messages, which could be useful for visually impaired users.

Recommendation: Our recommendation is to provide users additional forms of content creation, namely audio and video messages. Audio and video messages could be a potential way to make the request creation process easier for some of the elderly users. Furthermore, adding text-to-speech functionality can be very useful for reading out typed messages.

R8: Customization

Customization, where the power of choosing how elements might look or behave is given to the user, is an important tool in many digital applications. This

---

[15] https://robertsspaceindustries.com/roadmap/progress-tracker/teams/.

recommendation is mostly useful for the more feature rich platforms, like ¿Tienes Sal?, Hoplr, and Nextdoor that offer a myriad of options to their users. It is unclear how popular some of the added features on these platforms are, but in the case of P4 it appears from our user survey that at least older users might not use all of them. Nonetheless, access to these features does clutter the homepage and makes it more difficult for a user to find what he is looking for.

Recommendation: Our recommendation is to allow users to customize their main entry page. The customization does not need to be very complex and simply allowing a user to hide certain buttons might be enough. Ideally, the customization option could be coupled with the onboarding (R4), where users are shown all or most of the features and asked which ones they would like to keep or hide. Of course, by hiding features there is the risk that some features are used less. If many users are hiding a specific feature, it can be seen as an indicator that there is a need to improve the feature or consider removing it.

R9: Transparency (Trust and Security)

In our interview with P5, it became clear that some elderly users are starting to become more aware of data privacy and want to know how their data is protected and how it is used. All of the evaluated platforms are located within the EU and thus declare to follow the European GDPR (General Data Protection Regulation)[16]. GDPR lists a set of requirements aimed to protect users' rights in terms of data privacy. Because of this, the platforms do provide a generic data protection statement and Hoplr also mentions collaboration with ethical hackers, as well as providing some slightly more in-depth information on how data is used on their help page.

The raising awareness of users' need for data privacy could in part be due to a number of scandals reported about online social networking platforms, such as the Cambridge Analytica papers [3]. The COVID-19 situation also led to data privacy concerns with the release of contact tracing applications and the handling of a user's data [6].

Recommendation: A simple GDPR statement might not be enough to alleviate all concerns; instead *open and honest communication* on who is able to access or see the user's data is needed. Our recommendation is that platforms inform users clearly on how any information provided by the user is used by the platform. This could be coupled with recommendation (R3) Guiding or (R4) Onboarding, by integrating this information in the guidance or/and onboarding process.

R10: Support and Encourage Communication

The majority of the platforms leave it to the users on how to handle the inter-personal communication once somebody responded to a request. Usually, this follow-up is done by means of public or private chat messages. It is likely safe

---

[16] https://gdpr.eu/what-is-gdpr/.

to assume that for the majority of users this is fine as chat was rarely brought up as a grievance in our surveys. However, adding explicit support for other common forms of communication, such as phone, email, and popular external communication services, could be useful especially for elderly users.

We also noted a rather low level of internal chat use on all three surveyed platforms (P1, P3 and P4). In the case of P1 and P3 both surveys had a nearly identical level of inactive users (who had not used the main feature of the platform) and therefore did not need the chat. In P4's case, the results did vary somewhat depending on whether the participant had offered or asked for help, but on most occasions around half of the participants responded negatively on using private messages. Similarly, more older users had used the feature distinctly less. Additionally, having a possibility of keeping a family member updated on the activities of an elderly user could be a beneficial feature in the context of social support and safety. Of course, this brings additional privacy concerns to the table, but this is a feature that could be activated separately as needed, it would not be needed by a large group of users.

Recommendation: We have several recommendations for communication that we have split into two distinct sub-facets: *supporting communication* and *encouraging communication*.

Our recommendations for supporting communication are to provide more familiar means of communication (email, phone) and to couple them with the recommendations (R3) Guiding and (R4) Onboarding, as it is equally important to make users aware of these possibilities. Coupling support for email and phone, in terms of technical challenge, would be rather small for the platforms.

Our recommendations for encouraging communication: (1) Sending an automatic message via the chat to introduce the users to this feature. (2) Akin to P3's onboarding upon account activation, suggest sending a greeting message to other users. (3) Allow certain people to keep track of activities of their family members; making family members aware of a user's activity in the platform (e.g., via email, or another messaging tool) could be meaningful and increase feeling of social support and safety in the elderly.

R11: Help Manuals

The platform should provide technical support to their users and overall all of the platforms do accomplish this. At least, in so much that they do provide instructions for users by means of separate information and help pages. What we can conclude from the interviews, is that for most parts, elderly users seem to rely on direct in person connections when they get stuck. How easy an online help service is for the elderly is unclear.

Recommendation: Our recommendation is providing a leaflet that contains clear instructions of all the core features and how to use them, as well as a brief explanation about the platform itself.

R12: User Roles

Recruiting users and giving them different roles, has been used by online forums and social networks to lessen the need for expensive personnel. In the case of larger social networks this is likely the only feasible way for them to work. Outside this, providing users a distinct role within the platform can in itself be a source to be more engaged with the platform and its community.

Currently, out of the evaluated platforms, Nextdoor, ¿Tienes Sal?, and Hoplr do utilize user roles: Moderators (Nextdoor), Super users (¿Tienes Sal?), Volunteers & City Representative (Hoplr). To our knowledge, Commu and Nappi Naapuri currently do not utilize any user roles.

Recommendation: Adding user roles can be useful to 1) have a better control over created content once the platform reaches a certain size, 2) keep certain users more engaged with the platform, and 3) activate otherwise potentially dormant users. Our recommendation is to investigate from what types of user roles a platform can take advantage of. For instance, Nappi Naapuri and Commu might benefit from local representatives that broadcast area-relevant information or requests. More closed neighborhood platforms might not benefit from nigh all powerful admins, but rather from users that check the content of notifications and can highlight them if necessary. For instance, ¿Tienes Sal? and Hoplr could benefit from roles like event organizer or users who indicate points of interest in the area, or adding a more dynamic discussion angle between a neighborhood and the local municipality.

R13: Safety Features

In terms of current safety features to protect users against misuse of trust when helping people, the platforms largely rely on providing guidelines, such as meet outside in a public area. No inbuilt features otherwise are provided. Reporting users directly to the service provider was the most common safety feature.

It appears that for most parts, the encounters that took place based on requests formulated in the evaluated platforms, have been without any major incidents so far. This could partly be due to the small size of the platform user base, lack of actively meeting other users, or simply not being reported. Security when meeting unknown people is an important factor for most users but even more for elderly who might feel vulnerable, especially if the helper is expected to visit their home.

Recommendation: In terms of safety features, the features that we recommend are simple and relatively easy to implement, however they would require more volunteers. One such feature could be to announce an upcoming meeting to a third party. This could even be coupled with (R10) Support & Encourage Communication where a selected family member or even simply the platform is informed about the upcoming meeting. If both users are aware of this, it could work in making participants feel safer. Another option could be to invite a third party to join the meeting, but this would require available volunteers willing to join meetings and might require some calendar options to ensure that everyone is available.

Another safety feature would be to review encounters by attaching some form of feedback system for encounters. Also, some steps could be added to the help request flow, such as allowing both volunteer and requesting person to view more information on each other before sending a message.

Although being able to review encounters is a rather obvious recommendation, it however raises additional questions, for instance: Who may see those reviews?; How to avoid false bad reviews?; Should the review be anonymously?. Nonetheless, it could be a valuable avenue to help users assess for themselves whether meeting another user for the first time is a good idea, or not.

R14: Area of Visibility

This recommendation focuses on the platforms with closed neighborhoods (e.g., ¿Tienes Sal?, Hoplr, and Nextdoor). Tying the platform to a certain neighborhood can improve safety and security and should definitely be kept as such but it has the disadvantage that people outside the neighborhood cannot help, while a person from further away might be perfectly willing to help with a task, for instance because it is on his way to work. ¿Tienes Sal? already allows publishing notifications outside a users' own district to be seen in the neighboring ones.

Recommendation: Our recommendation is to allow some notifications, such as help requests, to be seen outside the user's neighborhood. Note that such a feature would require additional user instructions, i.e., to mark the message as visible outside the neighborhood, for instance by means of a color code.

R15: Provide Platform Activities

Especially P1 and P3 appeared to have a rather large number of dormant users. Reasons for these might vary. Generally, users can be grouped into four distinct categories 1) visitors, 2) passive members, 3) socializers, and 4) content generators [1]. In our interview, P3 stated that they had seen some success in reactivating users at least briefly with emails, but whether long-term engagement could be achieved was less certain.

Recommendation: Our recommendation is to provide simple, easy to do tasks or activities within the platform. Ideally, the user should be rewarded for performing the task or activity in some manner. Example tasks could be clearing old requests or reviewing new requests. Of course, giving users any rights over moderating messages is something to be considered carefully (as the interviews showed). This could be achieved by providing User Roles (R12) that might be useful for the platform's functioning and interesting enough for the user. Note that some of the user roles might not necessarily require social interaction, which could be attractive for some users. This type of engagement could turn dormant users into active ones, or keep some users who might otherwise not use the platform, suitably engaged.

R16: Registration

In the evaluated platform, creating an account (registration) varies in difficulty from simply typing some basic information to a multi-step verification process. This was clearly indicated as a stumbling stone for elderly users in our interviews with P2 and P4. The reason for having a registration feature is clear, as it aims to increase trust in the members within the community, as the user needs to give its details.

Recommendation: We have three intertwined recommendations for this purpose: Firstly, the registration process should be as easy as possible with very clear fields and ideally minimal input required.

Secondly, a two-step registration process could ease the likelihood for elderly and other users to join the platform by allowing access to basic functionalities without a location verification. To alleviate registered users' security concerns, content created by non-registered or verified users could be color coded or categorized separately. This opens up an avenue to possible problems, such as spamming or bots. It means that some features might need to be restricted for not fully registered users, but this is a matter of discovering the optimal balance.

Thirdly, circumventing the use of classic passwords could also be a strong booster for elderly users, either by using third party login services, such as Google's, by email, SMS authentication codes, or authentication services such as itsMe[17] or bankingID[18]. It is important to consider the trade-off between safety and easiness, and there is plenty of evidence that traditional passwords might not be very safe, mainly because of the users themselves [7].

5   Conclusions

In this paper we have proposed 16 design recommendations for social engagement platforms. These recommendations are based on the results of evaluating several social engagement platforms. The platforms were evaluated thoroughly by means of a hands-on evaluation, interviewing representatives of some of the platforms, as well as user surveys. The goal of these recommendations is to make social engagement platforms more accessible to elderly users and to improve retention. Our recommendations are useful for existing social engagement platforms to improve their solutions as well as when developing new platforms. A limitation is that the recommendations have only been evaluated in a limited way, i.e., by asking the opinion of representatives of platforms and users. To evaluate our recommendations in detail, a long-term user study with a platform implementing the recommendations might form part of our future work.

Acknowledgements. We would like to thank the representatives of Commu, Nappi Naapuri, Hoplr, ¿Tienes Sal?, and Solidare-it! for their valuable cooperation during the realisation this research project.

---

[17] https://www.itsme.be.

[18] https://www.nordea.fi/en/personal/our-services/online-mobile-services/code-app.html.

References

1. Akar, E., Mardikyan, S.: User roles and contribution patterns in online communities: a managerial perspective. SAGE Open **8**(3) (2018). https://doi.org/10.1177/2158244018794773

2. Baddeley, M.: Hoarding in the age of COVID-19. J. Behav. Econ. Policy **4**(1954), 69–75 (2020)

3. Cadwalladr, C., Graham-Harrison, E.: Revealed: 50 Million Facebook Profiles Harvested for Cambridge Analytica in Major Data Breach (2018). https://www.theguardian.com/news/2018/mar/17/cambridge-analytica-facebook-influence-us-election

4. Cascaes Cardoso, M.: The onboarding effect: leveraging user engagement and retention in crowdsourcing platforms. In: Extended Abstracts of the ACM Conference on Human Factors in Computing Systems (CHI 2017), Denver, USA, pp. 263–267 (2017). https://doi.org/10.1145/3027063.3027128

5. Cox, B.: The Power of Onboarding: Building Persuasive User Experiences for Companion Apps. Expert View, pp. 1–4 (2021). https://www.ondrugdelivery.com/

6. Fahey, R.A., Hino, A.: COVID-19, digital privacy, and the social limits on data-focused public health responses. Int. J. Inf. Manag. **55** (2020). https://doi.org/10.1016/j.ijinfomgt.2020.102181

7. Florencio, D., Herley, C.: A large-scale study of web password habits. In: Proceedings of the 16th International Conference on World Wide Web (WWW 2007), Banff, Canada (2007). https://doi.org/10.1145/1242572.1242661

8. Froehlich, M., Kobiella, C., Schmidt, A., Alt, F.: Is it better with onboarding? Improving first-time cryptocurrency app experiences. In: Proceeding of the International Conference on Designing Interactive Systems (DIS 2021), pp. 78–89. Online Event (2021). https://doi.org/10.1145/3461778.3462047

9. Lindberg, R.S.N.: Design recommendations for social engagement platforms: towards enhanced technology adoption for elderly people and long-term engagement. Ph.D. thesis, Vrije Universiteit Brussel, Brussels, Belgium (2022)

10. Lindberg, R.S.N., De Troyer, O.: Towards an up to date list of design guidelines for elderly users. In: Proceedings of the 1st International Conference of the ACM Greek SIGCHI Chapter (CHI Greece 2021). Online (2021). https://doi.org/10.1145/3489410.3489418

11. Martinho, D., Carneiro, J., Corchado, J.M., Marreiros, G.: A systematic review of gamification techniques applied to elderly care. Artif. Intell. Rev. **53**(7), 4863–4901 (2020). https://doi.org/10.1007/s10462-020-09809-6

12. Nguyen, H., Nguyen, A.: Covid-19 misinformation and the social (media) amplification of risk: a Vietnamese perspective. Media Commun. **8**(2), 444–447 (2020). https://doi.org/10.17645/mac.v8i2.3227

13. Sauer, P.: Latvia is First Country to Reimpose Lockdown in Europe's new Covid Wave (2021). https://www.theguardian.com/world/2021/oct/20/latvia-enters-month-long-covid-lockdown-as-fourth-wave-breaks

14. Strahm, B., Gray, C.M., Vorvoreanu, M.: Generating mobile application onboarding insights through minimalist instruction. In: Proceedings of the International Conference on Designing Interactive Systems Conference (DIS 2018), Hong Kong, pp. 361–372 (2018). https://doi.org/10.1145/3196709.3196727

15. Villius Zetterholm, M., Lin, Y., Jokela, P.: Digital contact tracing applications during COVID-19: a scoping review about public acceptance. Informatics **8**(3), 48 (2021). https://doi.org/10.3390/informatics8030048

16. Volkmann, T., Miller, I., Jochems, N.: Addressing fear and lack of knowledge of older adults regarding social network sites. In: Gao, Q., Zhou, J. (eds.) HCII 2020. LNCS, vol. 12209, pp. 114–130. Springer, Cham (2020). https://doi.org/10.1007/978-3-030-50232-4_9
17. Zhang, S., Jiang, H., Carroll, J.M.: Integrating online and offline community through Facebook. In: Proceedings of the International Conference on Collaboration Technologies and Systems (CTS 2011), pp. 569–578 (2011). https://doi.org/10.1109/CTS.2011.5928738

Experimentation of a Nighttime Wandering Assistance System Based on AAL Solutions to Foster Aging at Home

Hubert Ngankam$^{(\boxtimes)}$, Hélène Pigot, and Sylvain Giroux

Laboratoire DOMUS, Département d'informatique, Université de Sherbrooke, Sherbrooke, Canada
{hubert.ngankam,helene.pigot,sylvain.giroux}@usherbrooke.ca
https://domus.recherche.usherbrooke.ca/

Abstract. To promote the aging in place of elderly people with cognitive impairment, it is desirable to make their homes more intelligent. With Ambient Assisted Living (AAL) systems, it is possible to define intelligent environments that can take into account the needs of these people. This article presents the results of the experimentation of a Nighttime Assistance System (NAS) for elderly people with Alzheimer's disease. The NAS uses AAL technologies to non-intrusively monitor the Activities of Daily Living (ADL) of an elderly person living alone, to contextualize and adapt the help that will be offered to them. For this experiment, we collected data for five weeks on a person's activities. This work describes how this experimentation was carried out with an emphasis on user needs. It also shows the different patterns of activity observed, with particular emphasis on nocturnal ambulation. Finally, it describes the contextual model set up to support the person in the event of an episode of nocturnal wandering.

Keywords: Ambient assisted living · Nighttime wandering · Context awareness · Ubiquitous computing · Alzheimer's disease

1 Introduction

Context refers to any information that can be used to characterize the situation of an entity, knowing that an entity can be a person, a place, or a physical object [3]. To facilitate aging at home and allow seniors to regain some autonomy in achieving some Activities of Daily Living (ADL), it is important to consider the context in which these people live. Taking into account the context of the assistance to the elderly makes it possible to better adapt the solutions of pervasive computing and ambient assistance. Above all, it offers the ability to these solutions to anticipate people's needs and to act accordingly. It is therefore important, to get contextual information on sub-tasks, places, sensors, actuators, and objects involved in an activity.

© ICST Institute for Computer Sciences, Social Informatics and Telecommunications Engineering 2023
Published by Springer Nature Switzerland AG 2023. All Rights Reserved
I. M. Pires et al. (Eds.): GOODTECHS 2022, LNICST 476, pp. 80–93, 2023.
https://doi.org/10.1007/978-3-031-28813-5_6

Several assistance solutions based on Ambient Assisted Living (AAL) and context awareness have been yet developed [5–8,10,29]. They are aimed to foster autonomy at home for seniors by providing environmental cues either to recall an activity to do or the way to perform it.

At night, people with Alzheimer are often experienced nighttime wandering that could provoke anxiety, temporal disorientation, and risks to fall. The contextual assistive system is therefore useful to create a calm environment that encourages people to go back to sleep. This article extends the NAS (Nighttime Assistance System) from [9,11], a non-intrusive AAL system that allows validating the elderly's profile by detecting needs and building appropriate environmental cues to overcome the episodes of nighttime wandering. The paper also presents the results of a five-week experiment that took place in the home of a senior with Alzheimer's disease. An embedded sensor network has collected data on actions, behaviors, and activities performed. To understand all its requirements, a context manager ensures that local and contextual exchanges are propagated throughout the NAS. Open-source middleware, rules-based system, and pervasive computing technologies are used to provide personalized, calm, and automated prompting for the elderly.

The rest of the paper is organized as follows: Sect. 2 discusses the related work; Sect. 3 describes the Nighttime Wandering System; Sect. 4 describes the sensor network and presents the results of the experimentation. Section 5 opens a discussion on the results obtained. Section 6 concludes the article.

2   Related Work

2.1   Smart Homes

More and more, we are witnessing a growing increase in the number of people aged 65 and over [1]. This has the direct implication that the percentage of older people who prefer to stay in their homes and communities is increasing rapidly. In general, this phenomenon is called "Aging in Place" [2]. It is possible to make this possible by using connected objects. Thanks to the Internet of Things (IoT), it becomes possible to transform all homes into smart homes. In this context, smart home technologies could significantly help people to have a better quality of life, to live independently, and to stay in touch with their family and caregivers.

Thanks to their software and IoT components, smart homes make it possible to collect data and thus monitor the state of health, behavior, and quality of life of elderly users, avoiding risky situations and putting users in contact with their family, caregivers, and medical staff [26,28,29].

In this type of intelligent environment, it is possible to find several heterogeneous IoT devices which, combined, offer the possibility of recognizing Activities of Daily Living (ADL) [4]. In [6,9,11,16], the authors proposed a platform based on the recognition of activities of daily living to enable seniors to age in place. Rashidi and Cook developed CASAS at Washington State University [29]. CASAS is an adaptive smart home that uses machine learning techniques to discover user behavior patterns and automatically mimic those patterns. User can modify automation policies, provide feedback on proposed automation activities and introduce new requests.

2.2 Ambient Assisted Living System

Deployed AAL systems deal with much contextual information, based on sensor/actuators information, user actions, user profiles, and ambient information such as humidity, temperature, and so on. The different technologies that accompany aging in place present several challenges:

- Facilitate communication between the elderly and caregivers.
- Monitor the health parameters of the elderly person.
- Monitor the environment and activities of the elderly person's daily life using sensors to ensure greater comfort and safety.
- Facilitate the mobility of people out of their homes.

To address those challenges, several mechanics are used [10,23,24,29]. Among those solutions, AAL middleware is mainly preferred to facilitate the homogenization of different technologies, while semantic approaches based on ontologies help represent different knowledge.

3 Nighttime Wandering System

The Nighttime Assistance System (NAS) [9,11] aims to detect the onset of episodes of wandering to assist during the night. It meets the needs associated with awakening and encourages people to go back to bed. It is designed using a ubiquitous and ambient approach to create an adaptive environment that is sensitive to the presence of a person. It requires a design approach centered on users, thus putting the technology in the background, giving way to assist in transforming their homes into smart homes. Several opportunities are offered by this approach to support older people to perform certain activities of daily living. Based on their life habits, it is possible to adapt the environment in which they live to their illness or age. To regulate the circadian rhythm proceeds, NAS works in two phases. The first phase, called the monitoring phase, involves the installation of a set of sensors in the home to gather the activities and habits of the person. The second phase, which is the assistance phase, offers personalized support based on the information collected. The NAS provides objective data on the behavior of the resident's home, which will be supported by physiological and subjective data collected from elderly people with Alzheimer's disease and their caregivers.

4 Experimental Assessment

This section presents a five weeks deployment of the augmented context-sensitive NAS. for several weeks in an experiment with a lady of 86 years old, living alone and suffering from Alzheimer's disease. Particular emphasis is placed on the creation of the contextual environment, the construction of functional modules, and their deployment at home. To better meet the needs of the person, four constraints had been set:

1. The solution must be pervasive and contextual for better monitoring of needs.
2. NAS could provide oral messages, but just when necessary.
3. At all times, the system monitors its status and can give information on the possible breaking.
4. Avoid any inconvenience to the person by making all deployed technologies non-intrusive and calm.

The home is a flat house composed of one open room divided between the living room and kitchen, and one bedroom. This experimentation has required 101 sensors distributed in 30 electronic devices and 4 actuators distributed in 3 bloom lamps and 1 sound system.

4.1   Methodology

This section describes how the Context Awareness Architecture, has been implemented. It focuses on creating and transforming the living space of the person into a smart space. This is a multi-contextual collaborative environment of the real world, with the individual and his needs at the center.

Sensor Installation. The first step is to make an inventory of the physical environment to identify the furniture, the rooms, and the habits in the daily use of certain objects, priority or non-priority movements in and between rooms, the use of household appliances and electronic devices. This process makes it possible to have complete cartography of the places and a precise idea of the organization and the disposition of the various sensors and actuators. This mapping is called the *SmartDomus*, that is, the smart part of the house that is subject to a continuous, contextual process of assistance.

Localization and Pervasive Identification. A smart home may understand, learn and respond to the needs of users. To do this, it must know what is happening. Sensors are used to collect environmental data in an ambient manner. Eleven Motion detectors are used to locate the elder when any movement is in a room. If there is no movement, several pressure sensors scattered on most chairs help to determine the presence of the person in the room. Figure 1 shows how part of the person's smart apartment was realized. This part is called *SmartDomus*.

4.2   Material and Methods

Every detail of the experiment has been readjusted to the requirements of the person. In this experiment, the basic scenario set up to satisfy the needs of the person was gradually updated to better take into account the specificities of the person. Two main phases have been used, with different levels of complexity and varied expectations. The following subsections show in detail the steps taken to determine the interactions between the sensors, the environment, and the system. The following table lists the different types of devices (sensors, actuators, controllers, computers) used for the experimentation. All the sensors are Z-Wave sensors to avoid wired sensors that necessitate breaking holes in the wall Table 1.

Once the room identification in the *SmartDomus* is complete, sensors must be physically and logically labeled. Physically, labels are affixed on each device according to the place where it will be installed. Logically, each sensor must be linked to the controller so that it can be associated with the same Z-Wave logical network whose controller is the main node. Generally, this association is done in the controller and can differ from one controller to another. For the sake of simplicity, the sensors have the same logical name as the physical ones.

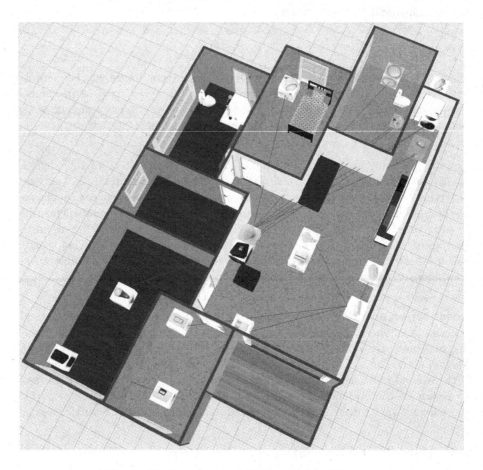

Fig. 1. The smart part of the house: *SmartDomus*

Table 1. List of equipment used for experimentation

Type/Room	Device - Action
Bedroom	Pressure - Lying - down/on
	Motion - Movement in the bedroom
	Contact - Door opening/closing
	Contact - Wardrobe opening/closing
Toilet	Pressure - Bathroom
	Motion - Movement in the toilet
	Contact - Door opening/closing
	Contact - Pharmacy box opening/closing
	Water detector - Flush toilet
Kitchen	Electric Measuring - microwave power
	Motion - Movement in the kitchen
	Contact - Door opening/closing
	Contact - Drawers opening/closing
	Contact - Fridge opening/closing
	Contact - Freezer opening/closing
	Contact - microwave on/off
Living room	Electric Switch - TV power
	Motion - Movement in the living room
	Contact - Door opening/closing
	Contact - Drawers opening/closing
	Pressure - Couch Lying/Sitting down/on
	Pressure - Armchair Sitting down/on
Outdoor	Motion - Movement in the veranda
	Motion - Movement in the staircase
Ambient information	Temperature
	Humidity
	Brightness
Actuators	Philips Hue Bloom Lamp - Cues
	Bluetooth speaker
Wearable sensor	Actigraphy - accelerometer
Controllers	Vera lite 3
	Philips Hue Bridge
	Arduino
Ranger	Extender Z-Wave module ranger
Computer	Computer Core I5

The Aeotec multisensor 4 in 1 sensor was used for motion, temperature, humidity, and light detection. Each drawer and door of the *SmartDomus* has been equipped with contact sensor type Everspring sm810 door/window contact. In sanitary facilities, water sensors have been installed to detect water flows. Aeotec water sensor has been used for this. For the detection of the presence of the bed or chairs water sensors have been hacked, to add several flexiforces mounted in parallel, as shown in Fig. 2. This transformation allows us to maintain a certain homogeneity in the Z-Wave protocol. All other diffuse information is collected by the sensors' brightness, temperature, and humidity sensors aeotec multisensor 4 in 1. Concomitant use of sensors will provide the system with the ability to search for the information needed to facilitate contextual assistance in *SmartDomus*.

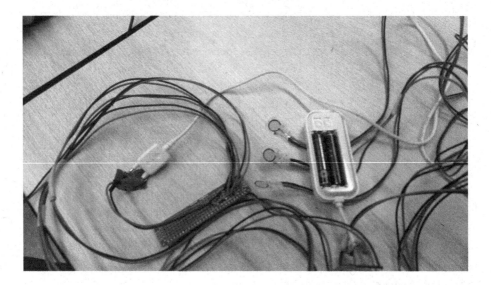

Fig. 2. Hacking the water sensor.

Profile Modeling of the Person. Before beginning the experiment, health questionnaires, dementia identification tests, and questionnaires on the needs and preferences of the person have been submitted to the elderly and also to her caregivers. Then, in a user-centric design, a custom scenario is created to offer support in the *SmartDomus*. This personalized information made it possible to learn that the person was no longer doing the dishes or preparing meals in the kitchen. It is then not necessary to install devices to detect the actions associated with these activities. We equip the elderly with wearable sensors, that is a bracelet containing an actigraph, which gives information about Profile modeling that begins before the beginning of the experiment, and then continues throughout the experiment. The experiment is divided into two phases. During the first phase, which lasts for 2 weeks, sensors are installed and send information about the habits during the night. The assistance scenario is then built based on the lifestyle habits collected. During the second phase of experimentation, which lasts for three weeks, modeling and profile rehabilitation meetings were held to refine the patterns identified in the activities of the person's daily life. For five weeks of experimentation, four follow-up meetings were conducted to verify and refine the person's profile.

4.3 Processing

To better take into account the heterogeneity of the data, a middleware that handles several communication protocols is installed. This middleware reads the data from the controllers, then formats them and transforms them for later use. For simplicity, we chose the **OpenRemote** middleware installed in a docker. This middleware written in Java makes it possible to make an inference using the rules-based first-order logic. For the persistence of data, a Postgres SAL DBMS is used. It is installed on a specific docker. The use of several dockers facilitates microservice management and scaling up. The docker-compose module facilitates the orchestration and management of the different dockers used.

The user-centric scenario design defines an inference mechanism that ensures that each assistance rule produced meets the requirements of the person's profile. The middleware provides an inference layer for writing these rules. For the sake of simplicity, simple rules are written and then aggregate to cover complex situations. This facilitates the use of an incremental and scalable method throughout the process. All written rules are tested on-site to ensure that they meet the needs of the person.

Raw data of each type of sensor and actuator are sent to the corresponding controller, here on vera lite 3, Arduino, and Philips Hue Bridge whenever an event occurs. The vera lite presents collected data of sensor events in standardized formats such as XML or JSON. The format of raw data is (deviceId, value). This represents a part of context acquisition. For example:

$$(244; on) - (125; on) - (20; on) - (25; 9.586) \qquad (1)$$

The labelization and contextualization transform them in the following sequence:

$$(ToiletRoomMotion_1; on)$$
$$(ToiletCarpetPression; on)$$
$$(ToiletWaterFlush; on)$$
$$(TVPowerMeter; 9.586) \qquad (2)$$

The processing context analyzes each of the information received, groups it by pattern, and then sends it to the reasoning context for the application of the assistance rules. At each iteration, the context of the person's profile is

consulted, and the relevant information associated with the current scenario is
therefore included in the treatment context. The label (2) becomes

$$if(ToiletWaterFlush == on \ \&\& \ ToiletCarpetPression == \text{off}) \ then \ action \tag{3}$$

Each pattern is translated by rules written in Drools language, where cron
jobs monitor the arrival of events. Figure 3 shows an example of a notification to
the person. This rule urges her to ask him to return to bed if she is up for 25 min
between 0 am to 6 am. Reminders are gradually displayed every 10 min if she is
not in her bedroom. An audio recording is played in case of complications. This
recording is the voice of a caregiver asking her not to go outside and reassuring
her before inviting her to go back to bed. Its operations are set up in the context
manager and the context processing. All this information is stored in a database,
iteratively and continuously in this vocal message.

```
rule "Nighttime wandering assistance in case of kitchen wandering "

    timer (cron: 0 25/10 0-6 * * ?)

when
        Event( source == "vSystemActive", value == "on" )
        Event( source == "HallMulti2Motion", value == "on" )
        Event( source == "RoomMulti2Motion", value == "off" )
        Event( source == "RoomMulti1Motion", value == "off" )

then

    execute.command("KitchenHue1On");
    playFile();
    sendMonitoringInformation(GLOBAL_INFORMATION, source);
    watchGlobalTimer();

end
```

Fig. 3. Partial view of nighttime wandering assistance rule.

To ensure the reliability of the system, a mechanism for managing faults and
errors is put in place. The system can inform about its status and indicates what
problems it encounters. In this case, a ping and pong program allows the set to
test the state of the controller and the middleware. In case of failures, an email
is sent to inform the caregiver about the situation. An additional layer has been
added to inform the remaining battery level (here 28% was chosen). Another
remote ping system is used to check the state of the local computer where the
application is installed. The middleware sends pong messages every 10 s in the
form of heartbeats to notify of its proper functioning. This information is stored
in a file, every 15 s a cron job reads this file. In case of problems, an alert email
is sent to inform about the state of the system to put a quick solution in place.

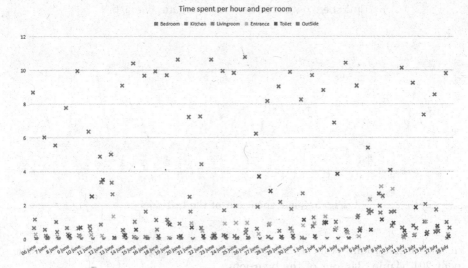

Fig. 4. Time spent per hour and per room between 8 pm and 8 am.

5   Results and Discussion

During all these 5 weeks, the system collected data continuously on 7/7 and
24/24. The data relating to the test days after the installation of the sensors and
after the installation of the actuators have been removed from the dataset. A
breakdown of electrical energy occurs for 1 day, leading to 2 days out of order. So
in total 5 days of data were excluded. The results presented in this section focus
on tracking the activities of the person during the night, that is, between 8 pm
and 8 am. A total of 1,827,789 entries were collected. After labeling and cleaning
(noise removal), synchronization, and network control information, membership,
in the *SmartDomus* during the experiment, the data went to 1 523 656 entries.
Then the restriction of night hours gives a total of 360 174 rows of data. Each
data line represents an event produced by the person and captured by a sensor.

Figure 4 shows the average duration of the senior's presence per room for
each night during the entire experiment. It shows that she spends more time in
her bedroom than in other rooms. We classify nights into three groups, group of
nights. The first group, the better night, is composed of nights of less than 6 h
spent in the room. Among others, there are 7, 8, 12, and 13 June. The second,
the average night is composed of nights about 8 h (6, 14 ...) in the bedroom. The
third group corresponds to about 10 h per night.

Figure 5 shows the time spent outside the bedroom in minutes per night. The
calculation is made from the moment the senior is lying on her bed and comes
out to satisfy any need. The notion of lying on the bed is defined as a continuous
period, the only activities observed are those on the bed. This calculation makes
it possible to observe the nights when she spent more time outside her room.
The graph shows that during the night of July 8 she spent 310.35 min, about

Time spent out of the beroom in minutes per night

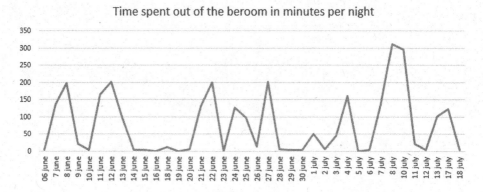

Fig. 5. Time spent out of the bedroom.

5 h, out of her room. Another relevant night is the night of June 12 when she spent 201.54 min, 3 h, out of the bedroom.

Number of exit out of the bedroom per night

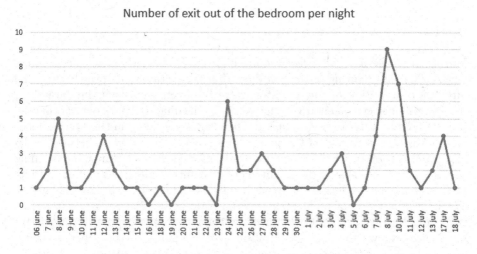

Fig. 6. Number total of exits out of the bedroom.

The time outside the bedroom is linked with the number of times she leaves her bedroom once she is lying down. Figure 6 shows the number of times per night she left the bedroom. Overall, it appears that this corresponds to past periods out of the bedroom. The diagram shows that on the night of July 8, she left her bed 9 times. Thus, Figs. 5 and 6 allow us to conclude that on the night of June 12 she left the bedroom 4 times, and was more than 201 min out of it. The night of July 8th shows that she has been out of the bedroom 9 times and has made more than 310 cumulative minutes out of the bedroom.

Based on the information collected, and the analysis carried out, a grouping of nights was proposed. Three categories have been identified. The first is the better night category, these are nights where the number of exits after the couch is less than 3 and the cumulative total duration of the exits is less than 30 min. The second category is corresponding to so-called average nights. An average night is a night whose number of trips is between 3 and 5 and the duration is less than 180 min. The last category is the bad night category, considered to be the one where the exit number is greater than 5 and the total duration is greater than or equal to 180 min. These criteria are suggestive and are suggested only based on observations made. Figure 7 shows the proportions of the different nights.

Representation of nights between 8 pm and 8 am

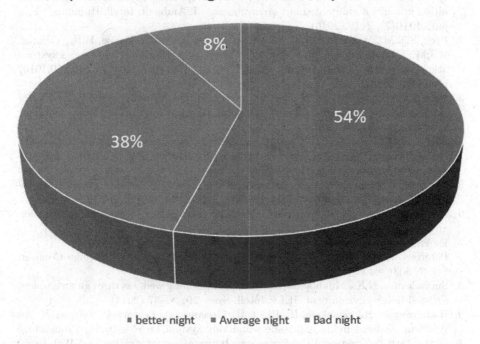

■ better night   ■ Average night   ■ Bad night

Fig. 7. Proportion of night.

According to these criteria, it follows that the percentage of average nights is quite high. Changing the cumulative total of times per exit can easily switch days from one category to another. For example, the transition from 180 min to 120 min for the average day's category will considerably increase its percentage. So these values are more influenced by the duration rather than the number of times she went outside her bedroom.

6   Conclusion

This paper described home-based experimentation. During several weeks, the non-intrusive and quiet system deployed collected through sensors and actuators information on the activities of the daily living of the person. The analysis and evaluation of the results show that the performance of the proposed architecture meets the requirements of context-aware systems. On the other hand, analysis of the data on the night activities makes it possible to understand nocturnal wandering behaviors from a data point of view. Experimental data revealed night patterns specific to the user.

References

1. Roy, N., Misra, A., Cook, D.: Ambient and smartphone sensor assisted ADL recognition in multi-inhabitant smart environments. J. Ambient. Intell. Humaniz. Comput. **2016**(7), 1–19 (2016)
2. Peek, S.T.M., Wouters, E.J.M., van Hoof, J., Luijkx, K.G., Boeije, H.R., Vrijhoef, H.J.M.: Factors influencing acceptance of technology for aging in place: a systematic review. Int. J. Med. Inform. **83**(4), 235–248 (2014). https://doi.org/10.1016/j.ijmedinf.2014.01.004
3. Dey, A.K., Abowd, G.D., Salber, D.: A conceptual framework and a toolkit for supporting the rapid prototyping of context-aware applications. Hum. Comput. Interact. **16**, 97–166 (2001)
4. Fahad, L.G., Khan, A., Rajarajan, M.: Activity recognition in smart homes with self verification of assignments. Neurocomputing **149**(PC), 97–166 (2015). https://doi.org/10.1016/j.neucom.2014.08.069
5. Charlon, Y., Bourennane, W., Bettahar, F., Campo, E.: Activity monitoring system for elderly in a context of smart home. IRBM **34**, 60–63 (2013)
6. Álvarez-García, J.A., Barsocchi, P., Chessa, S., Salvi, D.: Evaluation of localization and activity recognition systems for ambient assisted living: the experience of the: EvAAL competition. J. Ambient Intell. Smart Environ. **2013**, 5 (2012)
7. Peterová, R., Hybler, J.: Do-It-Yourself environmental sensing. Procedia Comput. Sci. **7**, 303–304 (2011)
8. Suryadevara, N.K., Mukhopadhyay, S.C.: Determining wellness through an ambient assisted living environment. IEEE Intell. Syst. **29**, 30–37 (2014)
9. Radziszewski, R., Ngankam, H., Pigot, H., Gregoire, V., Lorrain, D., Giroux, S.: An Ambient Assisted living nighttime wandering system for elderly. In: Proceedings of the 18th International Conference on Information Integration and Web-based Applications and Services (2016)
10. Blackman, S., et al.: Ambient assisted living technologies for aging well: a scoping review. J. Intell. Syst. **25** (2016)
11. Radziszewski, R., Ngankam, H.K., Gregoire, V., Lorrain, D., Pigot, H., Giroux, S.: Designing calm and non-intrusive ambient assisted living system for monitoring nighttime wanderings. Int. J. Percept. Cogn. Comput. **1**, 1
12. Hsia, P., Samuel, J., Gao, J., Kung, D., Toyoshima, Y., Chen, C.: Formal approach to scenario analysis. IEEE Softw. **11**, 33–41 (1994)
13. Forkan, A.R.M., Khalil, I., Tari, Z., Foufou, S., Bouras, A.: A context-aware approach for long-term behavioural change detection and abnormality prediction in ambient assisted living. Pattern Recognit. **3** (2015)

14. Kenfack Ngankam, H., Pigot, H., Frappier, M., Oliveira, C.H., Giroux, S.: Formal specification for ambient assisted living scenarios. In: Ochoa, S.F., Singh, P., Bravo, J. (eds.) UCAmI 2017. LNCS, vol. 10586, pp. 508–519. Springer, Cham (2017). https://doi.org/10.1007/978-3-319-67585-5_51
15. Schilit, B.N., Adams, N., Gold, R., Tso, M.M., Want, R.: The PARCTAB mobile computing system. In: Proceedings of the IEEE 4th Workshop on Workstation Operating Systems in WWOS-III, pp. 34–39 (1993)
16. Schilit, B., Adams, N., Want, R.: Context-aware computing applications. In: Proceedings of the First Workshop on Mobile Computing Systems and Applications, pp. 85–90 (1994)
17. Sohn, T., Dey, A.: iCAP: an informal tool for interactive prototyping of context-aware applications. In: CHI 2003 Extended Abstracts on Human Factors in Computing Systems, pp. 974–975 (2003)
18. Abowd, G.D., Dey, A.K., Brown, P.J., Davies, N., Smith, M., Steggles, P.: Towards a better understanding of context and context-awareness. In: Gellersen, H.-W. (ed.) HUC 1999. LNCS, vol. 1707, pp. 304–307. Springer, Heidelberg (1999). https://doi.org/10.1007/3-540-48157-5_29
19. Want, R., Hopper, A., Falcao, V., Gibbons, J.: The active badge location system. ACM Trans. Inf. Syst. 10, 91–102 (1992)
20. Gu, T., Pung, H.K., Zhang, D.Q.: Toward an OSGi-based infrastructure for context-aware applications. IEEE Pervasive Comput. 3, 66–74 (2004)
21. Hong, J.I., Landay, J.A.: An infrastructure approach to context-aware computing. Hum.-Comput. Interact. 16, 287–303 (2001)
22. Ma, T., Kim, Y.D., Ma, Q., Tang, M., Zhou, W.: Context-aware implementation based on CBR for smart home. In: WiMob'2005, IEEE International Conference on Wireless And Mobile Computing, Networking And Communications, vol. 4, pp. 112–115 (2005)
23. Bekiaris, A., Mourouzis, A., Maglaveras, N.: The REMOTE AAL project: remote health and social care for independent living of isolated elderly with chronic conditions. In: Universal Access in Human-Computer Interaction. Context Diversity, pp. 131–140 (2011)
24. Cook, D.J., Augusto, J.C., Jakkula, V.R.: Ambient intelligence: technologies, applications, and opportunities. Pervasive Mob. Comput. 5, 277–298 (2009)
25. Li, X., Eckert, M., Martinez, J.F., Rubio, G.: Context aware middleware architectures: survey and challenges. Sensors (Switzerland) 15, 20570–20607 (2015)
26. Perera, C., Zaslavsky, A., Christen, P., Georgakopoulos, D.: Context aware computing for the Internet of things: a survey. IEEE Commun. Surv. Tutor. 16 (2014)
27. Strang, T., Linnhoff-Popien, C.: A context modeling survey. Graph. Models. In: Workshop, vol. 4, pp. 1–8 (2004)
28. Kapitsaki, G.M., Prezerakos, G.N., Tselikas, N.D., Venieris, I.S.: Context-aware service engineering: a survey. Syst. Softw. J. 82, 1285–1297 (2009)
29. Rashidi, P., Mihailidis, A.: A survey on ambient assisted living tools for older adults. Biomed. Heal. Inform. IEEE J. 99 (2013)
30. Li, R., Lu, B., McDonald-Maier, K.D.: Cognitive assisted living ambient system: a survey. Digit. Commun. Netw. 1, 229–252 (2015)

Health

Improving the Recommendations of Meals in the PROMISS Application

Dewi Spooren[✉] and Laura M. van der Lubbe

Computer Science, Vrije Universiteit Amsterdam,
De Boelelaan 1111, 1081 HV Amsterdam, The Netherlands
dewispooren@gmail.com, l.m.vander.lubbe@vu.nl

Abstract. The PROMISS application is specifically built to let older adults keep track of their diet and protein intake. To improve the user-experience of this application, we study how machine learning algorithms can be used to recommend meals and products based on historical data. An intelligent workflow is designed which combines five different algorithms that recommend suitable meals and products. These algorithms are trained and tested using data from a previous user study with the PROMISS application. The change in user-experience is measured by the numbers of clicks needed to enter a meal in the application. Two different variants of the new application, namely, one using only the two new recommended meals and the other using both the two new recommended meals plus the old recommended meal, are compared with the old application. It was found that both new applications reduce the number of clicks and thus increase the user-experience of the application.

Keywords: Recommender systems · Diet tracking · Machine learning · Association rule learning

1 Introduction

Over the last few years, the usage of technology in the lives of older adults has increased significantly. An example of this is PARO: the famous seal that is used in elderly homes as a companion robot and a therapeutic tool. Research showed that the older adults were willing to interact with PARO and that this interaction improved their physical activity [12].

Technology can also be used in order to stimulate a healthy lifestyle, for example meal planning systems. Such an application has been created for the diet trial of the PROMISS project [17]. The PROMISS diet trial aims on increasing the protein intake of older adults with a relatively low protein intake [19]. One of the risks of a low protein intake is a rapid loss of muscle mass [10].

The PROMISS application is meant for daily usage during the diet trial. For each user, the application is personalized with the help of their personal diet plan created by the dietitians of the PROMISS project. Using a progress bar,

I. M. Pires et al. (Eds.): GOODTECHS 2022, LNICST 476, pp. 97–112, 2023.
https://doi.org/10.1007/978-3-031-28813-5_7

the total amount of protein consumed by the user is visualized throughout the day, helping the user complete their daily protein intake.

The PROMISS application that was used in the diet trail included meal recommendations based on the user's diet plan and previous input [17]. In this project the possibility of improving the user-experience by reducing the number of necessary clicks to enter a meal is studied. This can be achieved by creating an intelligent workflow using machine learning algorithms that personalize meal and product recommendations on regularities in historical data of users. Furthermore, it has been shown that using computer tailored information personalized on the user, is more effective in promoting a nutritious lifestyle, than general non-computer tailored information [11]. Thus, recommending meals in a more personalized way improves the user-experience not only by increasing the efficiency but also by making the recommendations more personalized.

First, background information about the PROMISS application and meal recommendation is discussed in Sect. 2. Second, the research methodology, including a description of the data, is described in Sect. 3. Third, the different algorithms are described in Sect. 4, together with an overview on how they work together. In Sect. 5 it is discussed how the training data has been determined. Finally, the conclusion and discussion can be found in Sect. 6.

2 Background

First, more details on the PROMISS application are discussed. Furthermore, an overview of related work on meal and product recommendation is given.

2.1 PROMISS Application

As mentioned in the introduction, the PROMISS application is a system to improve diet compliance for elderly users [17]. Protein points were used as a way to represent the protein value of products and meals. The users of the application could keep track of their diet by means of their protein points. The goal was to stimulate users to eat enough protein each day by providing them with a progress bar of the protein points they have gotten on a specific day or moment.

Before the diet trial, the eating habits of participants were monitored. Based on this information a diet plan, including the personal protein need, for each user was composed by a dietitian. For most participants, there were six eating moments per day: three main meals and three snacks. The diet plan consisted of one meal for each eating moment of the day, and it was the same for each day. The users each received a tablet with their personalized application. They were instructed to fill in meals they have eaten for each eating moment for a specific period of time. The original application contained three ways of entering meals:

– The user can enter a meal via the meal composer. They can replace, remove or add products from the recommended meal. When the user has switched a product for three times or more for the same product, the meal plan for that eating moment is adjusted by replacing the product.

- The user can directly enter the number of protein points eaten, without filling in the products of the meal.
- The user can use the additionally provided foodbox to register intake of specific products.

This system also had disadvantages. Firstly, each day the recommended meal was, in essence, the same. Secondly, when the user chose to deviate from the recommended meal, (s)he had to enter this meal manually. This can be a time depending task.

2.2 Meal and Product Recommendation

Technology is growing each day and is playing an increasingly larger role in our lives. Whether needed for work, sharing pictures on social media or downloading useful applications to make life easier, nearly everyone owns a mobile device [2]. Another thing that keeps growing is the problem of obesity and poor health. Being obese causes the death of over four million people each year [4]. However, it has been shown that obesity and health related problems can be prevented or even reversed in some cases through good nutrition [18]. Because of the growing use of technology and health problems due to obesity, there are quite some food recommender tools on the market which all try to stimulate a healthy lifestyle.

Elsweiler and Harvey presented an approach to integrating nutrition in a recommender system by grouping items, which together present a balanced meal, rather than recommending individual items [13]. During this experiment Elsweiler and Harvey gathered a taste profile of the participants, using data including recipes and nutritional properties, which users could rate. One potential pitfall was that the users did not rate enough breakfast recipes, and it has not been further researched how to improve the recommendation for breakfast meals.

Furthermore, the approach of Elsweiler and Harvey did not contain any research on the usage of the application by older adults [13]. The system 'Nutrition for Elder care' (NutElCare) by Espin, on the other hand, has been especially designed for older adults [14]. In the last few years, the usage of technologies among older adults has increased substantially. Which caused a higher willingness of using these kinds of technologies, such as food recommender systems, in their daily lives [14]. NutElCare uses knowledge-based techniques and requirements of the user to generate a recommendation of items. Furthermore, the user can rate meals which are used to calculate similarity scores between meals.

Many food recommender tools rely on the input from users. See, for example, work by Freyne and Berkovsky, whose recommender system use ratings on both recipes and food items [15]. Or the food recommender system from Professor Aberg, whose system uses collaborative filtering to predict a user's taste opinion on a recipe that the user has not yet rated based on other ratings [8]. Disadvantages of these systems are the lack of willingness of rating meals and the lack of rated meals for specific categories. No examples are found of systems that rely purely on historical data on eating habits of the users.

3   Method

This research studies whether personalized recommendations improves the user-experience of a diet tracking app. To do so, data from the PROMISS application used in the PROMISS diet trial is used. This data is described in the next section. The evaluation of the designed algorithms is explained in Sect. 3.2.

3.1   Data Usage

The data that is used has been gathered from the users that participated in the PROMISS diet trial [16]. The data has been anonymised in order to maintain the anonymity of the participants. When designing the five algorithms, the data of the protein products, the activity logging of the user and the day totals of the protein points is used. From the activity logging data, especially the data where the user fills in a meal using the meal composer are important for this research. This data contains all information (e.g. product and portion size) on the meals that are entered in the meal composer.

Furthermore, not all data of all participants is used. In the tablet study of the PROMISS diet trial, 36 participants were considered active users [16]. The data varies from 27 days as the least amount of data and 240 days as the most amount of data. However, some people did not use the meal composer for the majority of the time. They entered the number of protein points without the products their meal consisted of. Therefore, the percentage of meals entered using the meal composer has been calculated for each participant. It has been decided to use a threshold of 70% and only use data of users above that threshold. Further in this research, the 11 remaining participants are referred to as active users.

Subsequently, the period of training data has to be established. There needs to be a balance between having enough data which can lead to logical recommendations and containing the satisfaction of the user. During the training period there cannot be personalized recommendations based on historical data and thus this also needs to be taken into consideration. Until enough data is present, users are considered 'new users'. In the results section is explained how the training period has been established.

3.2   Evaluation of the Task Completion Time

When evaluating the task completion time, the number of clicks when entering a meal using the old application is compared to the number of clicks using the new application. As mentioned, this new application is improved through the use of five different algorithms which are explained in Sect. 4.

In Fig. 1, a screenshot of the meal composer in the old application is shown. On the left all products in the recommended meal are shown. When clicking on the blue button below the meal ('add a new product'), the categories of products appear on the right. By clicking on a category, the top 5 most used products for that user appear followed by all products in alphabetical order. By clicking on a product, this product will be added to the meal and the right part of the

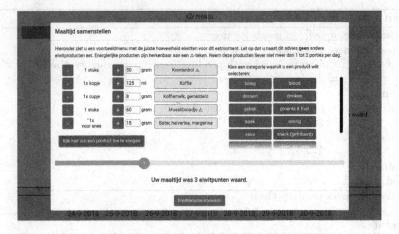

Fig. 1. Screenshot of the meal composer

screen is emptied again. Moreover, if a user wants to replace a product in the meal, (s)he can click on that product and all products from the same category will appear, with the right amount so that it contains the same protein value as the original product. In Algorithm 1 it can be seen how the number of clicks is acquired using the old application.

For evaluating the number of clicks for the new application, the test data is used to acquire the chosen meal. From the logging data of the user, it can be determined what products have been added or deleted to the recommended meal, this way the chosen meal can be acquired. Furthermore, the two personalized recommended meals obtained using the newly created algorithms are used. For the evaluation, the meal that resulted in the least number of clicks is used. A difference between the old and the new application can be seen in Algorithm 2: adding a product can also lead to two clicks when a product is chosen from the predicted product list which is acquired using a machine learning algorithm named association rule learning. When comparing the number of clicks

---

Algorithm 1. Pseudocode number of clicks old application
1: Initialize a recommended meal for user
2: **if** user replace/add product **then**
3:     **if** product can be replaced with product from same category **then**
4:         Clicks += 2
5:     **else**
6:         Clicks += 3
7:     **end if**
8: **end if**
9: **if** user removes product **then**
10:     Clicks += 1
11: **end if**

Algorithm 2. Pseudocode number of clicks new application

```
 1: Initialize recommended meals for user
 2: if user replace/add product then
 3:     if product can be replaced with product from same category then
 4:         Clicks += 2
 5:     end if
 6:     if product is in advised product list then
 7:         Clicks += 2
 8:     else
 9:         Clicks += 3
10:     end if
11: end if
12: if user removes product then
13:     Clicks += 1
14: end if
```

---

between the old application and the new application, a two-sided test for the null hypothesis that two independent samples have identical average expected values is conducted. The test assumes that the samples have identical variances.

4   Implementation

Five different algorithms have been designed and composed together such that it creates an intelligent workflow. The code of the algorithms and the evaluation of the algorithms can be found on GitHub [1]. The algorithms are implemented in Python 3.7.6 [5]. In this section, an overview of the general workflow and a description of the five algorithms is given.

4.1   Overview and General Flow

The basic working of the five algorithms is as follows:

- The **preset algorithm** computes the 10 most used presets from all active users. In this context, a preset is a combination of categories which often occur together. From these categories the algorithm creates a meal by looking at the most used products within these categories.
- The **protein points algorithm** is only used for meals filled in for dinner and the evening snack. The algorithm looks at how much points the user has still left for that day and recommends a meal within a range of these points.
- The **core + addition algorithm** considers products which are often used together in one meal. From this, one core of two products is chosen. Furthermore, the additions are products that appear in the same meal as the core. Combining the core and some additions, one meal is created.
- The **preference algorithm** is used to recognize people with a vegetarian or a pescatarian diet. Where vegetarians exclude both meat and fish from their diet, pescotarians do eat fish but not meat. This knowledge can be used to match their recommended meals with their preference.

– The **association rule learning algorithm** is used when the user decides to add or replace a product. Machine learning is used to discover relationships between the products from the current composed meal and all products in the database. These relationships can be used to predict the next product.

Figure 2 shows how the five algorithms are combined into one intelligent workflow. The colors which appear in the flowchart each advocate a different algorithm. The preset and protein algorithm have been combined together, which later is explained in detail.

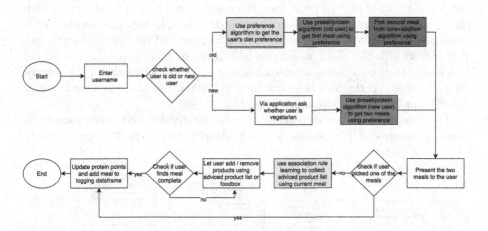

Fig. 2. Flowchart of general workflow

The first step of the flowchart is to enter a username to decide whether the user is an old or a new user. This is a crucial step, because the data used in the algorithms is different for new and old users. New users do not have historical data which can be used by the algorithms. In total there are two recommended meals. First, for old users, the preference algorithm is used to acquire the diet preference of the user. Then the two meals are deducted using a combination of the preset/protein and the core + addition algorithm. Both algorithms take into account the diet preference. The preference algorithm cannot be used for new users, hence the question whether the user's diet is vegetarian or pescatarian is asked. The two meals for new users are deducted using only the preset/protein algorithm and taking into account the diet preference.

Subsequently, the two meals are presented to the user. The user can add, replace or remove products from the recommended meal. In order to speed up this process, products are predicted using the association rule learning algorithm. This algorithm is used to acquire relationships between the products present in the meal and all the products in the database of the application. Based on these relationships a product is recommended to the user.

4.2   Preset/Protein Algorithm

The preset/protein algorithm is used to recommend the first meal to old users and to recommend both meals to new users. However, the working of the algorithm is slightly different for old and new users. Figure 3 shows the workflow of this algorithm. The first step in the flowchart is to retrieve the eating moment which the user wants to enter a meal for, this is due to the fact that for the eating moment 'Avondeten' (dinner) or 'Tussendoor avond' (evening snack) the protein algorithm is used and in other cases the preset algorithm is used.

Assume the flow for the protein algorithm is followed, both the data of the user's day totals of protein points and the protein need is used in order to gather the amount of protein left. If this amount needs to be split between the two eating moments, then 'Avondeten' uses 75% of this amount and the 'Tussendoor avond' 25%. Afterwards the check whether a user is old or new occurs, because if the user is old, their own meals are used in order to gather all meals for the specific eating moment. If the user does not have this data, meaning the user is a new user, the meals of all active users is used.

The meals for the specific eating moment are divided into clusters using K-means clustering. This machine learning algorithm clusters data by trying to

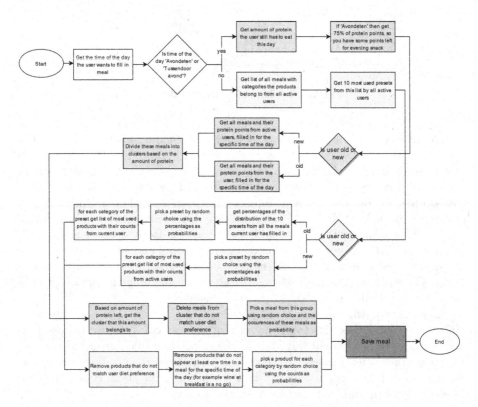

Fig. 3. Flowchart of preset/protein algorithm

separate samples in groups of equal variances (using [7]). It requires the number of clusters to be specified, therefore a range between 2 and 40 has been chosen and for each number of clusters k-means is used. The best silhouette score is commonly used as a factor to determine the appropriate number of clusters. For each cluster number the silhouette coefficient is calculated and plotted (using [3]). Using this plot, the highest silhouette coefficient is determined and therefore the appropriate number of clusters. Subsequently, based on the amount of protein left, it is decided which cluster is closest to this amount. The meals from this cluster are then examined whether they match the user's diet preference, and the occurrences of the meals are gathered. These occurrences are used as probability in order to choose a recommended meal using a random choice method [6].

For the other eating moments, the flow from the preset algorithm is followed. Presets are categories of products which often occurs together in the eating pattern of each user. For a Dutch person this could be the standard AVG (Aardappelen - starch, Vlees - meat but also includes fish/veggie, Groenten - greens) meal. The algorithm transforms each meal from all users for a specific eating moment into a list of the categories of the products. The 10 most used presets are selected. The approach on how to retrieve the recommended meal is different for old and new users.

If the user is old, the distribution of the presets in their own meals is calculated. The distributions are used as probabilities in order to choose a preset using the random choice method. For each category of the chosen preset, the most used products are gathered from all eating moments. Next, with a similar method a product is chosen for each category. The products that do not match the users diet preference are deleted. The products that do not appear at least one time in the specific eating moment are also deleted. Using the occurrences of the most used products in the meals from the user, one product for each category in the preset is chosen using the random choice method again. By adding all products together, the recommended meal is assembled.

If the user is new, so the user has not finished their training period yet, the distribution of the presets in all the meals of all users is used in order to choose a preset using the random choice method. Subsequently, the most used products for each category are gathered using all active users. From this moment, the algorithm continues the same as before. This way, users without historical data also receive a recommended meal.

4.3   Core + Addition Algorithm

The core + addition algorithm is used to recommend the second meal to old users. The preset algorithm can be used for new users, using data from all active users, however the core + addition algorithm is not modelled to be able to do this. Therefore, this algorithm is only used for old users.

According to the flowchart in Fig. 4 the first step in this algorithm is to collect all unique meals the user has filled in for a specific eating moment. From the unique meals, all unique two-product combinations are gathered. The combinations that do not match the user's diet preference are deleted. For each unique

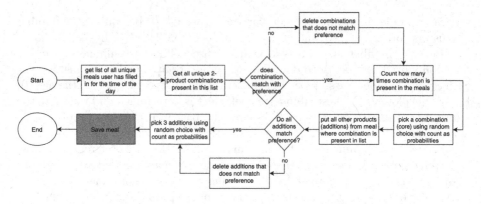

Fig. 4. Flowchart of core+addition algorithm

two-product combination, the occurrences in all meals from the specific eating moment from the user is collected. Using the occurrences as probabilities, one core is chosen using the random choice method. Subsequently, the algorithm goes through each meal from the specific eating moment where the core is present and gets the occurrences of all additions (consisting of one product) from these meals. The additions that do not match the user's preference are deleted. At last, three additions are collected using the random choice method and their occurrences as probability. The three additions and the core together form the recommended meal.

4.4   Preference Algorithm

The preference algorithm is important for both the preset/protein algorithm and the core + addition algorithm. The algorithm predicts the diet preference of the user and therefore prevents that recommended meals for people who eat vegetarian or pescatarian contain meat or fish products. This algorithm can only be used for people who have historical data, namely the old users.

First, as is shown in Fig. 5, the algorithm collects all the meals the user has filled in and checks for every meal whether all products in the meal are vegetarian or pescatarian. Beforehand it has been decided for every product in the protein products database whether a product is vegetarian, pescatarian or neither. If the percentage of vegetarian meals is above 99%, then the user's preference is vegetarian, this is the same for a pescatarian preference. The threshold of 99% is chosen because it would be a pitfall if the threshold is not high enough and thereby will wrongly delete meat or fish products from a user's recommended meal who mainly but not entirely eats pescatarian or vegetarian. However, 100% is not used, as sometimes participants might eat something that does not match their diet preference, but still have this as a preference.

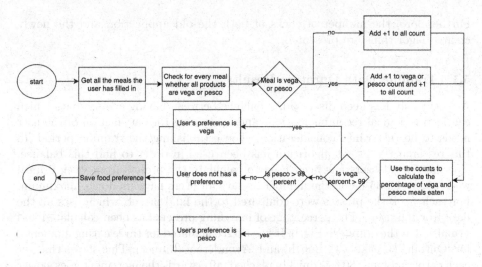

Fig. 5. Flowchart of preference algorithm

4.5   Association Rule Learning Algorithm

The application is not only improved on the part of recommending meals, but also when the user chooses to alter the recommended meal by adding products. As can be seen in Algorithm 1, it takes the user three clicks for adding a product which is not from the same category as the product the user wants to replace. In order to reduce this to two clicks, the association rule learning algorithm is used. In Algorithm 2 it can be seen that when a user wants to add a product which is in the advised product list, it takes the user only two clicks.

There are different software implementations of the association rule algorithms. This research uses the Apriori association rule algorithm created by Christian Borgelt [9]. It proceeds by identifying the frequent individual items in a database, hence it is chosen to use this algorithm in order to improve the addition of products. The Apriori implementation uses transactional data and generates frequent item sets from within this data in order to create association rules from these item sets [20]. An antecedent is an item found within the data, in this case a product or combination of products, a consequent is an item found in combination with the antecedent. In the algorithm where Apriori has been implemented, a list is created including all consequents with a minimum support of 0.05. The support is then used as probability and using random choice two consequents are collected. For at most 5 randomly chosen products present in the current meal, their 5 consequents are collected and presented to the user, which can help them choose products for their meal.

5   Results

As mentioned in Sect. 3, the available data has been split into training and test data. This section discusses how the training period has been established.

Furthermore, the number of clicks of both the old application and the newly created algorithms are presented.

5.1   Training Data Duration Results

As previously has been discussed, a balance between having enough data which can lead to logical recommendations and containing the satisfaction of the user needs to be taken into consideration when establishing the training period. In this research the preset algorithm has been used in order to find this balance. The data of all users has been used to calculate the presets from week 0 until week 35. Week 35 being the number of days all users have used as a maximum. For each week the presets were compared to the final preset, which uses all the data from all users. The percentage of matching presets has been calculated and visualized in the graphs in Fig. 6. It has been calculated for three eating moments, for 'Ontbijt' (breakfast), 'Lunch' and 'Avondeten' (dinner). This shows that for each eating moment 80% is quickly reached, afterwards the increment goes slower until it reaches 100%. For both lunch and dinner, the 100% mark takes a lot of time to reach. It makes sense in order to maintain the satisfaction of the user, to not choose 100% as a threshold. Taking lunch into consideration it is best to continue to 80%. It can be concluded that 80% is the right percentage, according to the graphs each eating moment quickly increases until 80%. Therefore, it has been decided to use 80% as a threshold, which means the training period is 10 weeks since the presets for lunch reaches this threshold at 10 weeks. Because of this, not all data can be used to evaluate the number of clicks, since some participants did not fill in meals for the whole training period. Moreover, some participants are excluded as bugs in the application makes their data unreliable. Thus, the remaining data that is used in for this study are from 7 users.

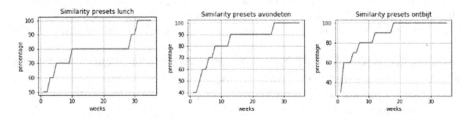

Fig. 6. Similarity scores for presets 'Ontbijt', 'Lunch' and 'Avondeten'

5.2   Results on the Number of Clicks

Algorithm 1 and Algorithm 2 show how the number of clicks can be calculated for the old and new application. In this section the results of the number of clicks are shown. For the new application, two different approaches have been used. First,

Table 1. Comparison number of clicks old application and both new applications.

	Breakfast (n = 81)	Morning snack (n = 61)	Lunch (n = 41)	Afternoon snack (n = 13)	Dinner (n = 43)	Evening snack (n = 12)	All meals average
Old	4.8 (SD = 4.32)	6.7 (SD = 5.06)	10.1 (SD = 6.81)	5.4 (SD = 3.11)	9.62 (SD = 4.55)	3.66 (SD = 3.60)	6.71 (SD = 4.57)
New (2)	2.8 (SD = 3.47)	4.1 (SD = 5.56)	7.88 (SD = 5.56)	4.8 (SD = 3.26)	7.15 (SD = 4.18)	4.08 (SD = 2.33)	5.135 (SD = 4.06)
New (3)	2.16 (SD = 2.77)	3.72 (SD = 4.94)	7.2 (SD = 5.54)	4.6 (SD = 3.36)	6.33 (SD = 3.86)	2.9 (SD = 1.76)	4.48 (SD = 3.71)

Table 2. Comparison p-value and t-test old application and both new applications.

		Breakfast (n = 81)	Morning snack (n = 61)	Lunch (n = 41)	Afternoon snack (n = 13)	Dinner (n = 43)	Evening snack (n = 12)	All meals average
New (2)/Old	p-value	0.004*	0.026*	0.126	0.627	0.093	0.74	0.269
	t-test	2.904	2.247	1.545	0.492	1.698	−0.336	1.425
New (3)/Old	p-value	8.715^-05*	0.004*	0.048*	0.475	0.005*	0.325	0.142
	t-test	4.028	2.969	2.01	0.726	2.87	1.007	2.298

the new application including the two meals resulting from the preset/protein algorithm and/or the core + addition algorithm. Secondly, a new application including three meals is evaluated. The third meal is the meal recommended in the old application and the two meals are the same as in the other new variant.

In Table 1 the mean average and the standard deviation of the number of clicks are shown. In the first row, the number of evaluated meals is presented. Looking at this table, it can be concluded that for each eating moment, the new application results into a lower number of clicks. Except for the eating moment 'Tussendoor avond': only the new application using three meals is lower than the number of clicks of the old application. Furthermore, the number of average clicks (M = 4.48, SD = 4.06) is even lower using the application using three meals than the application using two meals.

In Table 2 the results from the t-test comparing the new and old applications are shown The p-values which are significant (p < 0.05), are indicated with an asterisk. The majority of the p-values of the new application using three meals are statistically significant. For example, the participants who filled in a meal for 'Ontbijt' (breakfast) and used the new application using three meals (M = 2.16, SD = 2.77) compared to the participants who used the old application (M = 4.8, SD = 4.32) demonstrated significantly better scores (p-value = 0.004).

6   Conclusion and Discussion

To improve the user-experience for a diet tracking app, this research aimed to reduce the number of needed clicks to enter a meal in the application. As a use case we used the application that is used in the PROMISS diet trial and the data that is gathered during that study. The results show that it is possible to reduce the number of clicks by improving the recommendation of meals/products. For most of the meals, this reduction is significant. The application using three recommended meals performs even better than the application using two recommended meals. Logically this can be explained by the fact that because it includes the same meal as the old app, the number of clicks can never be higher.

However another explanation of why the application using three meals performs better is the case that the chance of a recommended meal which matches the users meal, increases when the number of recommended meals rises. It could be that adding more meals even reduces the number of clicks further because of this chance. However, displaying this in a user-friendly way is challenging due to the limited screen size of a tablet or smartphone. With the previously studied version of the application [16] it was found that the elderly users were successfully able to use the application. With only a limited change to the lay-out of the meal composer, to include three menus instead of one, we do not think that this will change. However, it is important that, before using it in a live setting, we test the new lay-out with users from the target group.

In this research historical data from a previously performed study was used. However, using live data might give different results, for example for the association rule learning algorithm. For example, the order of deleted or added products could not be taken into consideration in this research, but this could lead to a different list of advised products, which could lead to a higher or lower number of clicks. Furthermore, it could be interesting to take the time of scrolling for products into consideration. This is also an important factor for the time spend on the task of entering a meal, and thus could further effect the user-experience.

Moreover, when the new application will gain users, the number of active user's needs to be set to a specific number of users which represent the whole population. When dealing with new users, both the protein and the preset algorithm uses data from active users in order to create a recommended meal. When the number of active user's rises, this could take too much time. Further research could investigate an appropriate number of users which represent the whole population of users.

This research shows that an intelligent workflow for recommending meals and products within a diet tracking app reduces the number of clicks needed to enter a meal. Although other measures such as time needed for scrolling could not be taken into account due to the lack of a live experiment, this research provides a first step in making a more intelligent diet tracking system that can be used in interventions or trials.

Acknowledgement. This work was supported by the European Union Horizon2020 PROMISS Project 'Prevention Of Malnutrition In Senior Subjects' (grant agreement no. 678732).

References

1. GitHub Dewi Spooren - food-recommendation. https://github.com/dewispooren/food-recommendation. Assessed 1 July 2021
2. How many smartphones are in the world? https://www.bankmycell.com/blog/how-many-phones-are-in-the-world. Assessed 21 June 2021
3. Matplotlib: Visualization with Python. https://matplotlib.org/stable/index.html. Assessed 1 July 2021
4. Obesity. https://www.who.int/health-topics/obesity#tab=tab_1. Assessed 21 June 2021
5. Python 3.7.6. https://www.python.org/downloads/release/python-376/. Assessed 1 July 2021
6. Python library Random. https://docs.python.org/3/library/random.html. Assessed 1 July 2021
7. Scikit Clustering. https://scikit-learn.org/stable/modules/clustering.html#k-means. Assessed 1 July 2021
8. Aberg, J.: Dealing with malnutrition: a meal planning system for elderly. In: AAAI Spring Symposium: Argumentation for Consumers of Healthcare, pp. 1–7 (2006)
9. Agrawal, R., Mannila, H., Srikant, R., Toivonen, H., Verkamo, A.I., et al.: Fast discovery of association rules. Adva. Knowl. Discov. Data Min. **12**(1), 307–328 (1996)
10. Baum, J.I., Wolfe, R.R.: The link between dietary protein intake, skeletal muscle function, and health in older adults. Clin. Nutr. Aging (2017). https://doi.org/10.3390/healthcare3030529
11. Brug, J., Oenema, A., Campbell, M.: Past, present, and future of computer-tailored nutrition education. Am. J. Clin. Nutr. **77**(4) (2003). https://doi.org/10.1093/ajcn/77.4.1028s
12. Chang, W.L., Šabanovic, S., Huber, L.: Use of seal-like robot PARO in sensory group therapy for older adults with dementia. In: 2013 8th ACM/IEEE International Conference on Human-Robot Interaction (HRI), pp. 101–102. IEEE (2013). https://doi.org/10.1109/hri.2013.6483521
13. Elsweiler, D., Harvey, M.: Towards automatic meal plan recommendations for balanced nutrition. In: Proceedings of the 9th ACM Conference on Recommender Systems, pp. 313–316 (2015)
14. Espín, V., Hurtado, M.V., Noguera, M.: Nutrition for elder care: a nutritional semantic recommender system for the elderly. Expert. Syst. **33**(2), 201–210 (2016). https://doi.org/10.1111/exsy.12143
15. Freyne, J., Berkovsky, S.: Intelligent food planning: personalized recipe recommendation. In: Proceedings of the 15th International Conference on Intelligent User Interfaces, pp. 321–324 (2010). https://doi.org/10.1145/1719970.1720021
16. van der Lubbe, L.M., Klein, M.C.A., Visser, M., Wijnhoven, H.A.H., Reinders, I.: Experiences with using persuasive technology in a diet trial for older adults. In: In The 14th PErvasive Technologies Related to Assistive Environments Conference (2021). https://doi.org/10.1145/3453892.3458686
17. van der Lubbe, L.M., Klein, M.C.: Designing a system with persuasive communication to improve diet compliance for elderly users. In: Proceedings of the 13th EAI International Conference on Pervasive Computing Technologies for Healthcare, pp. 234–241 (2019). https://doi.org/10.1145/3329189.3329217
18. Ornish, D., et al.: Can lifestyle changes reverse coronary heart disease?: the lifestyle heart trial. Lancet **336**(8708), 129–133 (1990). https://doi.org/10.1145/2792838.2799665

19. Reinders, I., et al.: Effectiveness and cost-effectiveness of personalised dietary advice aiming at increasing protein intake on physical functioning in community-dwelling older adults with lower habitual protein intake. BMJ Open **10**(11) (2020). https://doi.org/10.1136/bmjopen-2020-040637
20. Zheng, Z., Kohavi, R., Mason, L.: Real world performance of association rule algorithms. In: Proceedings of the Seventh ACM SIGKDD International Conference on Knowledge Discovery and Data Mining, pp. 401–406 (2001). https://doi.org/10.1145/502512.502572

Author Index

I. M. Pires et al. (Eds.): GOODTECHS 2022, LNICST 476, p. 113, 2023.
https://doi.org/10.1007/978-3-031-28813-5

Printed in the United States
by Baker & Taylor Publisher Services